Shri Abhilash Khandekar ji,

Eminent Journalist & a brother

with love & regards,

(Dr. D. Shella)
Penny Lall Sasher
8/3/2016

Future of India

Future of India

Dr. D. Bhalla

PRABHAT PRAKASHAN
ISO 9001: 2008 Publishers

Published by
PRABHAT PRAKASHAN
4/19 Asaf Ali Road,
New Delhi-110 002 (INDIA)
Tele : +91-11-23289777
e-mail: prabhatbooks@gmail.com

ISBN 978-93-5186-647-3
FUTURE OF INDIA
by Dr. D. Bhalla

Edition
First, 2016

Price
₹ 300.00 (Rupees Three Hundred only)

© Reserved

Printed at
R-Tech Offset Printers, Delhi

*To all my spiritual masters
who taught me the essence of life
and also taught me the inevitability of death
and who inspired me throughout and
to Maa Bhagwati whose blessings made
me what I am.*

President,
Global Research Alliance

R.A. Mashelkar, FRS
National Research Professor
National Chemical Laboratory
Dr. Homi Bhabha Road, Pashan,
Pune - 411 008. India

Chairman, National Innovation Foundation
Chairman, Reliance Innovation Council

Formerly
Director General,
Council of Science & Industrial Research

Secretary,
Department of Scientific & Industrial Research, Govt. of India

President,
Indian National Science Academy

FOREWORD

I found the book 'Future of India' penned by Dr. Bhalla as eminently readable, informative, insightful and enjoyable. Dr. Bhalla has spent more than 30 years of his life in public administration. His inside-out view rather than an outside-in view makes this book very interesting.

Dr. Bhalla puts India's dynamically changing position in the global setting in perspective first. There is an engaging and a detailed comparison with China. He rightly points out that India finds itself moving from the peripheral to the global-centre hub power position. There is an interesting discussion on the dynamics of this geo-political change, especially in the current VUCA world, which is volatile, uncertain, complex and ambiguous).

The author then takes us through a sectoral look at the Indian economy with a nice historical perspective of the past, a sharp analysis of the current and an interesting forecast of the future.

There is a good discussion on infrastructure, especially with respect to power and the oil and gas sectors. The various government initiatives in recent times have been highlighted as are our challenges and opportunities.

Dr. Bhalla lays a very heavy emphasis, and rightly so, on public-private partnerships (PPP). The government initiatives for promoting PPP, while enhancing the quality and quantity of PPP projects is then discussed. He seems to be a big champion of the PPP mode and recommends that it be used far more extensively in railways, higher education, power, urban infrastructure and health sector.

There is a good discussion on agriculture, while acknowledging our successes, the current pain points are also highlighted. Dr. Bhalla advocates that India must benefit from the potential of GM crops by creating promotional and precautionary policies. He gives an important alert on the question of food security, which I agree with fully.

The big challenge of rapidly expanding (rather exploding!) Indian urbanisation is then discussed. This is backed up by solid facts and figures. He advocates the method called DPTP, which means the development plan followed by town planning.

Then there is a good discussion on the health sector. The concerns about child malnutrition, sanitation, etc. as also the rapidly rising burden of non-communicable diseases are mentioned. Apart from affordability and access, the author rightly highlights the importance of awareness building. This is evident in the currently ongoing Swachh Bharat Mission also, where awareness and attitudes are going to play a bigger role than availability and access.

The all-important sector of education follows. From 'right to education', one must move towards 'right education'. Quantitative expansion must be accompanied by quality transformation. With emphasis on private sector participation, creation of global presence and international enrolment, the nexus between education, excellence, equity and employment has been rightly highlighted.

The book ends by making several positive recommendations on the way forward and shows how Indian growth and development paradigm can undergo a major shift with the right leadership and certain amount of boldness in thinking, decision-making and some out-of-the-box thinking leading to radical solutions, not just incremental ones.

Finally, having myself written the book 'Reinventing India' recently, I must say, I learnt a lot through this insightful view of the 'Future of India' penned by Dr. Bhalla. I hope numerous readers across India will enjoy it too.

R.A. Mashelkar
FRS

PREFACE

Having spent more than 30 years of my life in public administration, I thought this was the right time to pen my views and experiences of three decades, in the form of a book regarding the growth story in all sectors of India's economy. This book takes a look at India's future on an assumption that it's not just the big macro level policy changes that need a change, which in any case the respective Governments of the day will do, but that there is an inherent need to expedite the small things so relevant in each sector. Believe me; this can change the face of our Nation forever. So in that sense, this book is not intended to be a big treatise on India's Economy or its policies but seeks to reflect my views as a long standing Government functionary and citizen of this country on subjects which touch my heart. I strongly believe that this may have a bearing on India's future.

My objective in writing this book was to take the readers through the country's progress and its challenges in various sectors while at the same time making it an enjoyable reading. It's my feeling that if this work's widely read, it could touch a chord in the hearts of various sections, and when it does, the purpose would have been achieved. Nothing more, nothing less!

ACKNOWLEDGEMENTS

First of all, to all the government publications, books, libraries I have used including 'Google-Guru' helping my research.

Shailja Mendiratta, my skillfull niece, who despite her young age has a penetrating insight and did the content editing for the book throughout.

Sh. T.N. Ashok and Smt. Shimla, who did the editing of the book from time to time and gave some very useful suggestions.

Smt. Vatasala Joshi, Sh. Abhilash Khandekar, Sh. Ashok Wankhede, Sh. Milind Mahajan, Sh. Girish Gokhale, who had benefitted the book by their long and engaging conversations with me from time to time from which I drew a lot of material for the book.

To my batchmates of IAS 1986 batch who have contributed to my growth as well as to this book.

To my mother Smt. Kailash Bhalla and to my father late Sh. Jitender Nath Bhalla for having always believed in me.

To my wife Smt. Asha Bhalla *alias* Vishakha Dongre for her sacrifice of "time meant for her" and allowing me to devote that time to writing of this book.

To my sisters Sadhna, Vijay and Sangeeta and to all my daughters and sons who are not physically born to me but are my mental off-springs.

To my staff Jyoti Prabhakar, Jogesh Kumar, Sharawan Kumar and Ravinder Sharma who have contributed to this work from time to time.

To Sh. Atul Jain and Sh. Abhay Mahajanji from Deendayal Research Institute, for their faith and help.

And finally to my source of inspiration, *Smt. Sumitra 'Tai' Mahajan, the Hon'ble Speaker of Lok Sabha*, who has been a teacher, mentor and a mother and has shown me how to make difference in people's lives.

Lastly, I don't claim it to be an absolutely original work. Many thoughts, phrases, idioms or word-structures would have been that of others which I have expressed in my own language to present a core theme – where lies the 'Future of India'. So I acknowledge indebtedness to all such sources. Especially to Dr. Raghunath Mashelkar for writing a great foreword to this book and for inspiring me by his book 'Reinventing India'. I believe in what he said,

"Next century will belong to India, which will become a unique intellectual and economic power to reckon with recapturing all its glory, which it had in the millennia gone by. And I believe this will happen as the dawn of the new millennium turns into a morning, and what a glorious morning would it be for my India."

CONTENTS

Foreword — 7
Preface — 11
Acknowledgements — 13
1. India's Position in the World — 17
2. Indian Economy — 33
3. Infrastructure — 45
4. Public-Private Partnership — 61
5. Indian Agriculture — 69
6. Indian Urbanisation — 79
7. Health Sector — 83
8. Education in India — 90
9. Tourism – The Great Multiplier — 97
10. North-East – An Opportunity — 135
11. Last but not the Least — 164

INDIA'S POSITION IN THE WORLD

Hundreds of books may have been written on this topic with various authors taking extreme positions on either side of the pendulum. There is a section of people which believes that India is a global super power in the making. In fact in the eighties, a think tank in the United States came out with a treatise in its journal, "The Executive Intelligence Review", predicting that India would turn a Super Power in the late nineties and well into the new millennium. The report was carried by a leading wire agency and widely published in Indian newspapers and also overseas, caused some ripples in policy making bodies in the government raising eyebrows and hopes that this prediction would actually come true and that it was not some wild theory. The EIR had based this on some research on India's economy and growth story and projections that far reaching policies would be unveiled in the future. The EIR was not far wrong, because the 90's led to India opening up its economy and replacing the Red Tape with the Red Carpet for investors domestic and foreign. The policy changes effected by the then Narasimha Rao government under the then dynamic top economist turned bureaucrat turned politician Finance Minister Dr. Manmohan Singh in liberalizing rules and regulations for functioning in the country and throwing out archaic rules, that fettered progress, rapidly began to change the face of the country.

Now, when I talked about various authors taking different viewpoints, I had in mind some of those who would talk of demographic dividend and count hundreds of blessings in the form of opportunities coming India's way. Of course, some would say India is better than China or will be the best economy in the world by 2050. There is another section of people who are probably influenced by a tinge of pessimism to believe India's demographic dividend is actually going to be a curse because the nation is doing nothing to impart skills to its youth, so that they get meaningful jobs providing a satisfying livelihood to enable them to contribute substantially to the country's growth. They also believe that our infrastructure sector spanning banks, aviation, railways and logistics is in a poor shape and that it does not show any promise of quick change or turn around. They will also perhaps produce dozens of negative reports or factors in support to prove their view point. Actually, the truth lies somewhere in between these two extremes.

The world at present is characterized by massive production and financial systems spreading on a global scale. A universal revolution is on in computational and communication systems. There is a massive demographic change accompanied equally by a mega environmental disruption and geopolitical upheavals everywhere. If you look back, all this was foreseen much earlier, when the heads of more than 160 countries and Prime Ministers of an equal number of nations met at Rio De Janeiro in Brazil 33 years ago in 1992 to debate and formulate a concerted strategy under the auspices of the United Nations to come out with a historic document called the Agenda 21. India played a major role in the formulation of this document which lays down the basic tenets for sustainable development where the world is not ravaged by industrialization and its side effects in terms of pollution and a host of other problems. The North South divide was evident at the conference by some historic positions taken by the developing countries led by India and China and the developed countries led by the United States and Europe.

It is history that the bible of the conference 'Agenda 21' soon led to the establishment of a more permanent structure called United Nations Conference on Sustainable Development (UNCED). In fact the precursor to UNCED came fifteen year earlier at Stockholm Conference at Sweden when world leaders first addressed the issue of sustainable development and environmental degradation. India's then charismatic Prime Minister Indira Gandhi attended this historic conference and voiced India's concerns to the world.

In Rio, the member States decided to launch a process to develop a set of Sustainable Development Goals (SDGs), on which to build upon the Millennium Development Goals and converge with the post 2015 development agenda.

The Conference, one should recall, also adopted groundbreaking guidelines on green economy policies. Governments also decided to establish an intergovernmental process under the UN General Assembly to prepare options on a strategy for sustainable development financing. Governments also agreed to strengthen the United Nations Environment Programme (UNEP) on several fronts with action to be taken during the 67th session of the General Assembly.

In all these efforts, India was in the forefront and played a dominant part in protecting the interests of the developing world. It is interesting to note that 23 years later the United Nations re-enacted the Rio Conference with a summit on

Sustainable Development in 2015, in the same exotic city of Brazil, which is spearheading the BRICS group along with India, China, Russia and South Africa setting trading principles and standards outside the forum of the United Nations under the WTO safeguarding the interests of the developing world. India is the founding member of BRICS group which consists of developing and emerging economy's. BRICS countries are facing similar kind of problems. These are large economies and have large populations which represent 42% of world population. BRICS has been set up as independent International organisation to encourage commercial, political and cultural cooperation between BRICS nations on the principles of non-interference, equality and mutual benefits. Even a BRICS Bank has now been set up with a pool of funds contributed by each member of the group. The Bank named as New Development Bank or BRICS bank is to provide loan to developing countries to help finance infrastructure projects. President of the bank will rotate among member countries and the first President is from India. India has been in the forefront of dialogues and policies of this institution which "illustrates a new polycentric system of international relations" in comparison to the U.S. dominated institutions like World Bank and International Monetary Fund. The Prime Minister of India has proposed to establish BRICS Agriculture Research Center and even BRICS network university draft was agreed upon in principle during BRICS working group meeting on education in order to bring about a more focused cooperation between BRICS countries in the field of education.

The United Nations is now in the process of defining a post-2015 development agenda. This agenda is currently being elaborated through informal consultations of UN General

Assembly. The President of the General Assembly (GA) had appointed two Co-facilitators to lead these informal consultations. The process of arriving at the post 2015 development agenda is Member State-led with broad participation from Major Groups and other civil society stakeholders. Numerous inputs have gone into the agenda, notably a set of Sustainable Development Goals (SDGs) proposed by an open working group of General Assembly, the report of an intergovernmental committee of experts on sustainable development financing, GA dialogues on technology facilitation and many others. These are ambitious goals that have a bearing on the fate of whole humanity and even sustenance of the planet of which we all are inhabitants. The SDGs defined as "Transforming our world-The 2030 Agenda for sustainable Development" are: (i) End poverty in all its forms everywhere (2) End hunger, achieve food security and improved nutrition, and promote sustainable agriculture (3) ensure healthy lives and promote well being (4) ensure inclusive and equitable quality education and promote lifelong learning opportunities for all (5) Achieve gender equality and empower all women and girls (6) ensure availability and sustainable management of water and sanitation for all (7) ensure access to affordable, reliable, sustainable and modern energy for all (8) promote sustained inclusive and sustainable economic growth, full and productive employment and decent work for all. (9) Build resilient infrastructure, promote inclusive and sustainable industrialization, and faster innovation. (10) reduce inequality within and among countries. (11) Make cities and human settlements inclusive, safe, resilient and sustainable. (12) Ensure sustainable, consumption and production patterns. (13) Take urgent action to combat climate change and its impacts. (14) Conserve and sustainably use the oceans, seas and marine resources for sustainable development. (15) Protect restore and promote sustainable use of terrestrial eco-systems, sustainably mange forecasts combat deforestation and halt and reverse land degradation and halt biodiversity loss. (16) Promote peaceful and inclusive societies for sustainable development, provide access to justice for all and build effective, accountable and inclusive institutions at all levels. (17) Strengthen the means of implementation and revitalise the Global partnership for sustainable development. These are very lofty ideals and might appear even-topic but on these only depends the survival of future generations and the existence of mankind. India is fully committed to these goals and has extensively contributed towards the finalising of these goals especially to the goal on ocean eco-system which focuses attention on the future of Island States and also the goals related to environment, especially the climate change and sustainable consumption, as to live in harmony with nature and peaceful co-existence is the part of our traditions and culture. The well being of all people is the basic tenet of Indian ethos. In fact not only India is committed but even the development agenda of the present Government reflects the same goals.

Even the Intended Nationally Determined Contributions (INDC) submitted by India ahead of an annual climate change conference to be held in Paris is a comprehensive document. The major flagship programmes like, the smart cities Mission, Atal Mission for Rejuvenation and Urban Transformation (AMRUT) Swatch Bharat Mission, National Heritage City Development and Augmentation Yojana (HRIDAY), National Mission for clean Ganga, Soil Health Card Scheme and the Pradhan Mantri Krishi Sinchayee Yojana are linked to climate objectives and SDGs. India promises in their INDCs to cut emission intensity upto 33-35% by 2030 as compared to 2005 level; to produce 40% of electricity from non-fossil fuel based energy resources. India has reset the renewable energy targets to 175GW by 2022 including solar wind and biomass which is one of the most ambitious targets set by any country in the world. It's a conference the world is looking at keenly to align its growth oriented strategies to the guidelines set in there.

The conference would take a 2nd look at Carbon Emission standards that the North and South have been battling out through several international conferences. Developing countries have been contesting the standards saying that most of the pollution was caused by industrialised nations such as United States and leading ones in Europe. The same standards could not apply to developing countries which were far less industrialised. Climate change and its consequent problems are created mostly by developed nations like USA through their life style, consumption and industries. They should morally bear the cost of endeavors for offsetting the climate change generated crisis to ensure the 'climate justice' for the poor people of world: It is in this context that India talks of the common principle but differentiated responsibilities. The debate led to a system of carbon trading where nations causing less pollution earned grades that could be traded with other nations for their benefit to acquire greener technologies to put a cap on their carbon emissions.

Climate change and its effects on the ecology and environment due to pollution being created by industrialised nations have been and continue to be the core of discussion under UN forum between North and South. It is worth mentioning that, the United States of America and the People's

Republic of China, both having a major responsibility in combating global climate change, came to a historic understanding and agreement in 2014.

It was to this end, President Barack Obama and President Xi Jinping reaffirmed the importance of strengthening bilateral cooperation on climate change and working together with other countries, to adopt a protocol, another legal instrument or an agreed outcome with legal force under the Convention applicable to all Parties at the United Nations Climate Conference in Paris in 2015. Both have committed themselves to reaching an ambitious 2015 agreement that reflects the principle of common but differentiated responsibilities and respective capabilities, in light of different national circumstances.

The Presidents of the United States and China thus announced their respective post-2020 actions on climate change, recognizing that these actions are part of the long range effort for transition to low-carbon economies. The United States intends to achieve an economy-wide target of reducing its emissions by 26%-28% below its 2005 level by 2025 and to make best efforts to reduce its emissions by 28%. China intends to achieve the peaking of CO_2 emissions around 2030 and to make best efforts to peak early and intends to increase the share of non-fossil fuels in primary energy consumption to around 20% by 2030. Both sides intend to continue to work to enhance these measures over time.

It is historic for China to reach such an accord because it has emerged as a major power and its strength is based on its well organized and high tech manufacturing sector which is virtually feeding the world in terms of construction projects. No wonder Prime Minister Narendra Modi has had the foresight to launch the 'Make in India' campaign that seeks to jump start its manufacturing sector hit hard by global recession. Some say this strategy has come a trifle too late, but the argument is that, it's better late than never. India may never catch up with China in this sector for another decade, because China has gone miles ahead. **But India can still nurture some hopes to catch up in the not too distant future.** If one looks at the world economy today, Russia has self driven itself into oblivion, mainly because of its intrant stand on Chechnya and dealing with this country obliquely by covertly supporting the rebels. **This led to sanctions being imposed by the United States on Russia and its having a tough time coping with them. Russia's oil exports were sustaining the country's fortunes on the back of the unprecedented rise in prices of crude in a market controlled by the cartel of oil producing nations mainly from the Gulf under the umbrella of OPEC. But the US sanctions coupled with its cut down on crude imports and reliance on its domestic shale gas largely led to oil prices swinging southwards resulting in a historic nose dive. The sharp decline in oil prices and sanctions have virtually contributed to the bankruptcy of Russia.**

The climate change as already mentioned earlier will be the biggest crisis of earth along with depletion of natural resources. All in all, planet earth is extremely vulnerable to abrupt changes of all sorts. Conventional thinking is not going to provide any quick fire solution. The need of the hour is an out of the box approach leading to radical solutions emerging from tangential thinking. There is no other way except bringing in sustainability to coincide with developmental goals everywhere in the world.

Suddenly India finds itself pitch forked into a position where it has become the global Centre of power. It has become imperative for America and Japan to align with India in industrial and technological partnership on various fronts. **The bipolar power order of the yester years shared between the United States and the then undivided Soviet Union or USSR is no longer there. Also with the dismemberment of Soviet Union, when the world became unipolar, America became all powerful ostensibly acting as the universal policemen seeking to protect democratic rights of individuals in controlled or despotic regimes**. But the same mighty American power, though still existing, no longer remains the supreme one. The relative decline of American power has been compensated by the rise of European and Asian nations and mind you, their growth is not a threat to the security of America in any way, but only complementary to it on the economic front. Containing Russia was a successful strategy. But now containing China, which was never an ally of America, is not going to be an easy task. **China with vast mineral resources and unparalleled huge manufacturing sector has virtually become the fallback nation for several economies in Europe and USA which rely on it to rescue them from the staggering effects of the global economic crisis, meltdown and recessionary trends still haunting the world. China is a near US$ 5 trillion economy with an envious foreign exchange position of US$ 4.3 trillion unmatched by any developing country or even developed country of the world. But even this mighty dragon economy has begun to overheat and the world is very concerned by its slowdown.**

China's more than successful integration into the global economy with its liberalization policies enables its better adjustment in the international arena than Soviet Russia. China not being a democracy and also being a significant geopolitical rival of America in future; poses a big dilemma. There is no easy solution to this predicament. It is in this scenario that, India has a role to play as a bridge for both America as well as for itself, which was long recognized by then US Secretary of State Ms. Condoleezza Rice who felt that US must help India become a superpower to counterbalance China.

There have been, from time to time, comparison between China and India and talk about whether both of them were actually on their way to become super powers. Once upon a time, Martin Wolf had characterised India and China as premature super powers which means they were potentially the nations in the front ranking because of their size and were actually struggling to fight wide spread poverty and other developmental challenges. China has come out of that and has become world's largest manufactures and exporter of goods whereas India is still having its own paradox of duality which is huge poverty on one side and economic achievements on other side. While India can hope to become a great power, it still is having the chains of developmental challenges around it. It has the largest number of world poor, malnourished, uneducated etc. Since 2008, when the world faced its financial crisis, India has done extremely well. After China's slowdown, in growth terms, it is second only to China. Besides because of its strategic location it has the advantage of America and other powers viewing it as a counter balance to China in Asian region. But India must realize that it cannot compete with China because the two countries are in different orbits. While we can have strategic alliances with U.S., Japan or even Australia. We cannot afford to offend China or have fresh border conflict with them. Rather than containment of China India should certainly count on its soft power and have more friends not only in South-Asia but also in East-Asia and goodwill in the world all around. But this all depends upon a pre-supposition that India will continue to achieve rapid economic growth in next one decade. If that doesn't happen, India will not only lose its place as the supreme player in South-Asia region but also its place as counter balance to China.

India has been strongly advocating for reforms in United Nations and restructuring of the Security Council to reflect the current political realities in all forums, bilateral as well as multilateral. India's plea is that the world has changed tremendously from the time the U.N. was setup. The number of member States has grown many fold and threats to peace and security have become more complex, unpredictable and undefined. Prime Minister Modi is pursuing this goal most vigorously and has been mobilizing support from the likeminded nations and groups like G4 Group (India, Japan, Germany and Brazil, G-69, group of around 42 developing countries and committee of C-10 of the African Union. After decades of discussions, finally it has reached the stage of text-based negotiations, brightening the hope of becoming Permanent Member of United Nations Security Council. India is continuously and rigorously arguing that Security Council must be expanded to include world's largest democracies and voices from all the major continents in order to lend greater credibility and legitimacy to it and also to make it more representative and effective in addressing the challenges of the 21st Century.

India has its rightful claim to a permanent seat in the reformed and expended UNSC as India continue to be among the top troops contributing countries for UN peace keeping operations and participating in 10 out of 16 ongoing peace keeping operations. Without reforms and expansion, U.N. itself runs the risk of rendering itself irrelevant. By any objective criteria such as population, territorial size, GDP, economic potential, civilizational legacy, cultural diversity, political system and past and ongoing contributions to the U.N. activities India is a most rightful claimant for permanent membership in the reformed UNSC.

Keeping in mind India's growing economy and its new global position, there is this urgent need for rapid growth in all the critical sectors of the country, which would result into rising incomes, more employment and a generally raise standard of living for its population with increased purchasing power. This could lead to reduction in poverty, greater literacy with improved education, better health care through a larger network of public health centers and well equipped hospitals, eventually leading to a rise in the economy. However, it is quite clear that this high growth trajectory, if not accompanied by rising employment will pose a great danger to the country's integrated structure because inequity in incomes will lead to more insurgency and internal disorder.

What this means is that the benefits of economic liberalization in the country cannot stay restricted to a particular section in urban centers but have to cascade to a larger section of the population in the semi urban and rural centers as well. It's a pity that even after 67 years of independence, 41% of the population still remains unbanked as per a report of the federal bank, that is the Reserve Bank of India. The need of the hour is micro financing and all institutions dealing with this can provide succour. The Modi government has launched its own initiative through the Jan Dhan scheme, that is, opening up of bank accounts for a large section of the semi urban and rural population. As per

government data a strategy of more than 160 million blue accounts have thus been opened, an effort which has found place in the government book of records. The subsidies benefits to the students scholarship and cooking gas are already being transferred directly electronically to the bank accounts of the beneficiaries which leads to transparency and efficiency in subsidy distribution system.

So it's in this context one talks of internal disorder or rise of naxalism if benefits of economic liberalization do not reach all sections of population. This can be seen in rise of naxal movement in the last two decades leading to emergence of 'Red Corridor' in India. It is not that in last three decades, Govt. of India has not spent enough money on education and health care, but it has not translated into the expected benefits for the population by yielding the right kind of results. That is why there is a greater need to create more well-paid jobs for the youth everywhere and to bring the populations in the peripheries and fringes of the country on to the express highway of development. All this will not happen without a high level of urbanization, higher education, large infrastructure and more flexibility in labour dominated-market structures. All these things have to happen on the domestic front, if at all India has to play its rightful innings at the global level.

It is very tempting to compare India's growth with China's, say, in the last two decades. Whereas Indian growth in per capita income has been 4% to 5% China's rate has been almost double. China's success has been mainly because of its being a manufacturing hub of the world and India's growth has been led by the service sector largely dominated by the Information Technology sector. While, there has been a very large decline in poverty in China, the same has not happened in India to that extent. In fact India today is where China was at the end of the neo-fascist communist regime led by Mao. The faster pace of industrialization and urbanization in China has created its own problems like most polluted cities and river systems. China's growth and its problems do provide a good direction and also caution for India telling us that we need to make very large investments in infrastructure and raise our health care, public sanitation, education and R&D structures but out with loosing sight of environmental preservation. We also need to cover our skill deficits very fast. We need to bring more techno managerial people in Indian Administration and make governance more effective, otherwise we may have the problem of crony capitalism, high cost health care systems and huge levels of poverty. **The Modi government has moved in the right direction by setting up a skill development ministry. It is taking help from the German government which is a pioneer in establishing centers of excellence for skill development in the world. It is quite clear India has huge potential for becoming the next manufacturing power house after China. But that cannot happen unless India gets over its key handicap of poor public infrastructure. India also needs to look at the potential of tourism as a growth accelerator.** Tourism is peculiar in its scope as multiplier in the economy because it creates ripple effect in many sectors of economy like human resources development, infrastructure, financial systems, transportation, cultural sectors, rural amenities etc. Especially with the availability of innovative technologies and online social media with universal reach, it is no longer very difficult to create tourism anywhere with some good physical resources being available.

Any country's global position depends upon its internal as well as external security status. National security is no longer defined by the military might only. It also depends upon the economic power of the country as has happened in case of America and China, and yet, defense preparedness as well as strong grip over the internal law and order situation is a sine qua non for being a global power. So this also needs to be addressed by the Country to make it a real superpower. Lastly we can take solace in the fact that Indian democracy has survived for more than six decades. Moreover it is the federal structure and frame work that has become more legitimate and more decentralized than what it was in 1950. More States have been created. At over 20 plus the number of states in India has almost doubled since independence. The role of the Centre and States has become more or less institutionalized but insurgencies in North East, Jammu and Kashmir and Punjab and rising naxalism in the red corridor do represent a small failure on the part of Indian federal structure. **No doubt that the Modi government is now pushing for cooperative federalism where the states have more autonomy and powers especially in respect of taxation and other measures to raise their sustainability. There is no doubt that more and more financial empowerment of states will help the Indian nation in its quest for further growth. Also, to some extent the era of coalition politics in the last two decades has also enabled States to become more vocal and powerful, although it has also created some problems in terms of national security.**

Let's now take a sectoral look at where India stands today and what are its challenges. Let's start with the economy and see how it has shaped up over the last three decades with the advent of economic reforms under various political regimes.

❑

INDIAN ECONOMY
(Economy as it Evolved in 20 Years – Status and Challenges)

The face of India's economy actually started changing much before the team of the then Prime Minister Sh. P.V. Narasimha Rao and his Finance Minister Dr. Manmohan Singh embarked on the Indian version of glasnost (openness) and perestroika (reconstruction) on the country's economic front. Under the immediate preceding regime of the then Prime Minister Chandrasekhar, India was virtually pushed to pledging its gold reserves in its fortress of the federal bank RBI to demonetise its debts.

What happened when Rao and Singh unveiled economic reforms on the financial and infrastructure sector is history. But what actually started it all was the dynamism of the charismatic Prime Minister Rajiv Gandhi who along with the techy star Sam Pitroda set in motion the Telecom Revolution and the massive transformation of the Information Technology sector. Rajiv Gandhi solved the seeds of the economic transformation with the Telecom and IT revolution which transformed the communication landscape of the country. No matter how far you travel deep in India, you can easily communicate with the world. It's easy to find a cyber café equipped with the latest generation computers with internet, wifi, and telephone kiosks that can connect you within the country and also with almost every country of the world at affordable prices. It was Rajiv Gandhi's vision to align with the global economy substantially through increased computer penetration in the country. Almost everything in daily life was computerised and it saved time and money for both the government and the people.

The foundation stone so necessary for building on further opening up of the economy and reaching out to the world for attracting investments for growth had already been laid by Rajiv Gandhi. Unfortunately historians talk less about this aspect of India's economic revolution and more about economic reforms that came later.

What happened in the 90's was an amazing transformation of the country. This was principally achieved by the administration of Narasimha Rao who virtually gave a carte blanche to the reputed economist Dr Manmohan Singh to work out in detail the economic reforms that covered the important aspects of financial sector and infrastructure reforms. The financial sector reforms covered the banking and insurance sectors mostly. The norms were liberalised for attracting foreign investments both through the Foreign Direct Investment (FDI) and portfolio investments (FIIs) routes. India rightly focused on FDI which meant locking up foreign funds in long term projects for growth which actually prevented any capital flight as had happened in many South East Asian countries that faced near financial disasters. The percentage of FII investments particularly in the shares and scrips of companies in the principal stock exchanges BSE/NSE was much less but substantial enough to alter the economic fortunes of India. India too faced capital flight when financial institutions pulled out to migrate to other countries but there were enough safeguards to prevent any economic disaster.

What is noteworthy to mention is that the fundamentals that Rajiv Gandhi and subsequently Narasimha Rao had laid out in terms of liberalised economic policies were unalterable by any subsequent government irrespective of political ideologies. Fortunately for the country, whether it was the Congress under the UPA or the BJP under the NDA they had the same economic ideology and policies could only be given a further push and were not put in cold storage or stopped. So India saw a surfeit of economic reforms in various sectors that were to follow during the five year regime of BJP led NDA under the then Prime Minister Atal Bihari Vajpayee, then next with the UPA regime led by Congress under the original architect of reforms Dr Manmohan Singh at the helm as the Prime Minister.

The first five years of Dr Singh's regime saw the economy steadily growing reaching a record 7 to 8% growth even as the world was rocked by economic recession triggered by the Lehman brothers crisis in the United States that cascaded all over Europe and other economies. India and China were the only two Asian tigers insulated against the effects of economic depression from which still many countries are yet to recover in Europe, particularly Greece, which is causing further worries to the world. Even a debt-restructing plan for Greece seems to be going no where.

To come back to India and China; their cycles of growth were fuelled by different sectors. India's main growth came from the services sector especially the IT and IT enabled service sectors. Institutions such as TCS, Infosys, Wipro, HCL and a host of other home grown companies heralded India's worldwide dominance in the software sector servicing industries mostly in Europe and America leaving a large footprint there. But India's manufacturing sector was still lagging behind. Growth was stalled in the vital steel sector because steel companies in India had to make steel by importing the raw material iron at high prices when locally available ore was being exported to earn money. The steel industry faced yet another problem – cheap steel imports from China by some manufacturers. A new steel policy is in the offing from the Modi government – Modi had in fact in an oblique reference to the faulty steel policy said India needs to export textiles not cotton.

The automobile sector touted to be the hub of small cars of the world in India slackened because the global recession tapered external demand cutting into exports of India made vehicles by leading American companies such as Ford or GM and South Korean companies such as Hyundai and even home grown companies such as the TATA Motors. This sector is still grappling with piled up inventories and sagging exports especially in the small car segment though the luxury segment has shown remarkable growth defying all odds of tapering international and domestic demand and companies such as BMW, Mercedez, Audi, among others sold more vehicles than the small car makers and are now sitting on a huge cash pile.

This had more to do with the consumer preferences. An entire set of new generation was moving up the economic ladder particularly from the IT sector, migrating from small cars to bigger cars which fuelled the growth of the sedan and luxury segment. From hatchback to four door sedans and coupes was the shift. Automakers were quick to notice this trend and brought with it a virtual revolution with affordable sports utility vehicles (SUVS). Earlier SUVs were not available for less than ₹ 10 to 15 lakhs. Prices dropped drastically to an affordable range between ₹ 6 to 9 lakhs maximum.

Companies such as the French automaker Renault, which was struggling against competition from Japanese, American and South Korean automakers, made a somersault with its Duster and its partner Nissan with its Terrano. They set the trend for the growth of other automakers with Maruti's Ertiga, and so on. Mahindra's already had a strong grip on the market with their Scorpios, Boleros and Xuv 500 brands. TATA's dominated with their Safari. But what is the scenario now? Despite an explosive growth in the automobile sector, India still does not have enough roads and highways to make the vehicles move smoothly on the roads. Vehicular pollution is at its peak especially in the capital causing a host of respiratory ailments among the population. No doubt the petroleum refining companies such as IOCL, HPCL and BPCL have been raising the quality of fuel to send less residual matter into the atmosphere. Bharat 5 the equivalent of the Euro V emission standards are in the offing. Bharat 04 is now under implementation. Reducing the sulphur content in fuel is a daunting and challenging task for the refineries.

Coming to the infrastructure, the National Highways Authority of India which builds most of India's highways and arterial routes in the country and the Transport Ministry under the stewardship of Nithin Gadkari are pushing ahead for faster growth with more km length being added to the highways under a tight timeframe. This bodes well for connectivity. The recently drafted new civil aviation policy has been well received by industry experts and airlines. The main crux of the policy is significant expansion of the platform for new capacity to enter

"An open skies project", has been proposed outside a radius of 5000 kms. which shall remove all restrictions on the number of flights to and from various destinations across the world. This radius almost covers West Asia, South Asian Countries to the East, which is a fairly good coverage. Here the flying rights will be auctioned. The license fee which will accrue to the government will increase its revenue. Also the policy talks about increasing the FDI cap from 49% to above 50% which will allow strategic investment by foreign carriers, the benefits of further capacity expansion. It is not that the airlines have not expanded in India in last 10 years but there have been challenges regarding commercial viability and there were restrictions on capacity expansion. It will now be done away with. But some components of the policy which show inclination towards micro management approach may not be worth in the long term. There is still empty rhetoric on the controversial '5/20' Rule. There is need for a genuinely competitive environment. We also need to think afresh whether we should actually cross subsidized air travel. This has become an obsolete approach. But still the new policy is welcome and any measure for creating more capacity in aviation and infrastructure will have benefits for the country.

    An overall look at the economy shows that some time had been lost during the last days of the UPA regime under the Congress as it was hit by alleged scams in the Commonwealth Games, coal blocks allocation and the telecom sector in allocation of spectrum. Media referred to this as the period of policy paralysis in the government when policy decisions were not being taken and growth had slowed down consequently to less than 5% in GDP, fiscal deficit had mounted to over 4% of GDP and current account deficit was left gaping as imports exceeded exports. The rupee had taken a toss in its value against the dollar rising to as high as ₹ 65 against the greenback, oil prices had skyrocketed internationally dealing a lethal blow to the operations of Indian refining companies such as IOCL, the dominant player in the market, when prices jumped as high as US$ 100 to a barrel. IOCL's profitability was eroded as the oil import ballooned leading to foreign exchange outflow and subsidies on the other hand sustained on account of cheaper than market prices for kerosene and LPG cramped the operations of the country's largest oil marketing company. Even as talks were on to amortise their debts through oil bonds, India bounced back as oil prices began to fall mainly due to reduced demand for it from the major oil guzzler of the world, United States which was relying on locally extracted shale gas and oil. The dramatic fall in prices from the peak of US $100 a barrel some years ago to around US$ 60 a barrel today has led to tremendous fall in the oil import bill by billions. But still the government of the day does not take it easy. There is an earnest attempt to cut down on subsidies. One of the schemes is to slash subsidies on the domestic LPG cylinder used by large number of citizens of the country. Known as DBTL. The government has asked people who can afford to buy gas cylinders at market prices to surrender their subsidies. There has been a fairly good response to this. It is also prepared to not provide subsidised LPG to people with annual income of ₹ 10,000,00 and above.

There is a good foreign exchange reserve now at around US$ 380 billion marching towards US$ 400 billion mark. But we are still far behind China which has a foreign exchange reserve of US$ 4.3 trillion for an economy of an equal size of US$ near 5.0 trillion. While the new government led by Narendra Modi has turned the tide against the legacy of a previous regime that was virtually, as media claimed, paralysed by lack of decision making, yet the government faces lots of challenges. The government has to tackle inflation which is still hovering around 5% to 6%, fiscal deficit that needs to be reduced to less than 5% of GDP, current account deficit needs to be reduced drastically through larger exports (*this means making our exports more competitive in the international market by offering industry more incentives*), banking sector reforms. The slowdown in the economy has led the government to recapitalise banks by over ₹ 70,000 crore. The rising Non Performing Assets (NPAs) with some of the public sector banks is a cause for concern as it affects their profitability.

World is passing through a very bad economic phase. China's slowdown as I have discussed elsewhere appears a prolonged one. World is now looking at the possibility of deflation which is already happening in commodities like oil, metals, agriculture commodities etc. which may benefit to some extent, the nations which are importing these commodities and hurt exporters but then such benefit also has a price tag. It can lead to sustained deflation which can cause reduced economic activities. This is already visible from the forecasts of International Monetary Fund. Deflation can only be fought by reducing interest rates. But if interest rates are already close to zero as is the case everywhere except India, in that case no stimulus can work. The implication for India is that while imports may be cheaper, exports will also fall severely which will hurt our growth. This situation calls for very serious economic reforms for increasing efficiency and competitiveness without which we may also not survive.

Coming to financial management, for the first time in the history of independent India, the government of the day signed a memorandum of understanding with the federal bank that is the Reserve Bank of India, to keep inflation under check and money supply under tight control. The RBI has been prudent not to reduce lending rates even as the Industry has been demanding the same to kick start the economy by making borrowing cheaper.

The RBI has kept lending rates more or less constant to rein in inflation by exercising a tight control over money supply through the Repo rate. *(The rate at which RBI lends funds to state owned commercial banks)*. This has come at the expense of keeping deposit rates low, which virtually hits the domestic middle class, which seeks better avenues for investment and the retired 60 plus senior citizens category, the most hard hit on their savings, earning little for their livelihood in the sun set years of their life, which is going to be humongous in the next few years.

The most critical sector, the power sector has not grown in proportion to the demand. One of the challenges facing the government is to create or ensure uninterrupted gas supplies for power plants, most of which has been hard hit due to insufficient or no gas supply. A lot of power capacity was created by the southern based power developers on the combined cycle power plant mode, more popularly known as the CCPP. The wrangle over gas pricing between the government and a private petroleum crude explorer and refiner namely Reliance Petroleum, led to an uncertain situation where gas supplies were not assured from the offshore Krishna-Godavari basin in Andhra Pradesh. Result they were forced to import costlier feedstock such as naphtha to run the power plants which made it uneconomical.

Some of these power developers such as GVK and GMR are now in consolidation mode closing down non-profit centres as there was no rate of return on their investment for some time. Some of them had also acquired coal mines in Australia at hefty prices to ensure uninterrupted supplies of cleaner coal. These companies are set to be facing tremendous hardships. This is a big challenge for the government to get them on stream. In the first quarter of 2015, power companies such as Lanco, GMR and GVK have shown losses of more than ' 200 crore each and over.

Another major challenge is the threat that China poses on the IT front. India's mainstay for foreign exchange earnings has come from the IT software and IT enabled services. India's dominance was because of its superior ability to make software for a host of applications demanded by industries in Europe and America. China is reportedly upgrading its software technology and also hiring English teachers by the hordes to get over its major drawback in business communication and language skills.

To attract more foreign investors, the government of the day had promised to liberalise economic policies further and also keep in abeyance the provision of retrospective legislation on certain direct or indirect taxes. However cases in courts would take their normal time to a logical conclusion. This is related to a tax dispute between the Income Tax department and the Telecom service provider Vodafone when the former sought to claim retrospectively some taxes on the proceeds of sale of equity that virtually rattled foreign investors who started having a cautious look at India as a favoured investment destination. The Government has already decided to not to resort to such retrospective taxation.

The new Government's forward looking statements have restored investor confidence to some extent and even raised investment ratings by leading rating agencies. The Modi Government has been addressing this issue aggressively and meticulously to make India and easy place to do business under 'Make in India programme'. 'Make in India' is Government's flagship campaign to boost the domestic manufacturing Industry and attract foreign investment in Indian economy. It is aimed at making India a manufacturing hub and transforming India's economy. The Government is committed to creating favorable conditions for business and industry by removing the bottlenecks, simplifying the procedures, fast tracking approvals and clearances and rationalizing a number of FDI related policy issues. To say a few, expediting the regulatory clearances, increasing the validity period of industrial licensing and de-licencing of a number of defense items, liberalizing restrictions, online application for industrial licensing with 24 × 7 service, online tracking of environment clearances no retrospective taxation, rationalization of the capital gains tax regime for real estate Instrument Trusts, decision to defer the implementation of the General Anti Avoidance Rule (GAAR) for two years. However major taxation reforms in the form of GST Bill are pending before the Parliament.

The Government Policy of liberalizing FDI in key sectors to the Railways, Defence and Insurance and taxation reforms underway, have resulted in higher flow of Foreign Direct Investment going up by 40% during 2014-15 as compared with previous year's identical period. A World Bank supported assessment of the case of doing burners reflects that the State Governments are also interested in economic reforms surprising some of India's poorest States have been the most aggressive in pursuing reforms. It sugars very well for the growth and developing of the Indian economy.

Government in India has rightly recognised that for employment for youth, there is no other way except to increase manufacturing activities and this can only be done by providing the ease for doing business. The Government has fast tracked approvals and clearances for industrial projects and infrastructure along with making transparent allocation of key natural resources and spectrum etc. FDI regime has been further liberalised to allow more increase in foreign investments in sectors like Railways, Defence and Insurance etc. Financing devices like infrastructure bonds have been allowed and number of regulatory and taxation issues have been addressed. While all these have been done; still there are more serious reforms which are pending like labour reforms, corporate governance, reforms in power sector, need for large scale reforms in agricultural sector along with providing safety net for the farmers. All these are a must for two digit growth for India.

Foreign investor's confidence in India seems virtually restored with steady inflow of foreign exchange. Prime Minister Modi's aggressive foreign policy has also helped to garner greater international attention on India and his record visits to as many 20 countries in just a year has helped bridge the gap between India and countries abroad looking towards India as the next alternative to China.

While we have dwelt at length on the Indian economy, and its transition from a state controlled one to a real laissez faire economy with greater autonomy to public enterprises and incentives to private sector entities, yet one has to look at the state of infrastructure so essential to driving India's growth in the coming decades.

❑

INFRASTRUCTURE

Infrastructure actually refers to basic facilities and systems that serve a country, so necessary for its economy to function effectively and efficiently. This covers typically roads, bridges, tunnels, water supply, sewers, electrical grids, telecommunications, and so on.

Of critical importance to India's growth is its infrastructure sector and the most important component of this are the Power, Oil and Gas sector besides highways, ports, steel and the cement sector – the building blocks of the sector.

Let's take a look at the status of these critical sectors first:

Power Sector

The Power Sector or the utility electricity sector in India now has an installed capacity of 271.722 GW as the end of March 2015. Renewable Power plants, constituted 28% of this total installed capacity and the Non-Renewable Power Plants constituted the remaining 72%. The gross electricity generated by utilities is estimated at 1106 TWh (1106,000 GWh) and 166 TWh by captive power plants during the 2014–15 fiscal. The gross electricity generation includes auxiliary power consumption of power generation plants.

India has achieved the distinction of being the world's third largest producer of electricity in 2013 with 4.8% global share in electricity generation surpassing Japan and Russia.

In 2014-15, per capita electricity consumption in India was 1010 kWh with total electricity consumption (utilities and non-utilities) of 938.823 billion kWh. Electric energy consumption in agriculture was the highest (18.45%) in 2014-15 among all countries.

Yet, the per capita electricity consumption is lower compared to many countries despite cheaper electricity tariff in India.

Official figures show that the installed captive power generation capacity (above 1 MW capacity) in the industries is 47,082 as on 31 March 2015. Another 75,000 MW capacity diesel power generation sets (excluding sets of size above 1 MW and below 100 KVA) have also been installed in the country. Also, there are innumerable DG sets of capacity less than 100 KVA to cater to emergency power needs during power outages in all sectors such as industrial, commercial, domestic and agriculture.

Of the 1.4 billion people inhabiting the globe with virtually no access to electricity, India accounts for over 300 million. The International Energy Agency estimates India will add between 600 GW to 1,200 GW of additional new power generation capacity before 2050.[This additional capacity is said to be equivalent to 740 GW of total power generation capacity of the European Union (EU-27) in 2005. The technologies and fuel sources India adopts, as it adds this electricity generation capacity, may make significant impact to global resource usage and environmental issues.

Some 800 million Indians use traditional fuels – fuel wood, agricultural waste and biomass cakes – for cooking and general heating needs. These traditional fuels are burnt in cook stoves, known as *chulah* or *chulha* in some parts of India. Everyone knows that the traditional fuel is an inefficient source of energy, it releases high levels of smoke, PM10 particulate matter, NOX, SOX, PAHs, polyaromatics, formaldehyde, carbon monoxide and other air pollutants.

Some reports, including one by the World Health Organisation, claim 300,000 to 400,000 people in India die of indoor air pollution and carbon monoxide poisoning every year because of biomass burning and use of chullahs. Traditional fuel burning in conventional cook stoves releases unnecessarily large amounts of pollutants, between 5 to 15 times higher than industrial combustion of coal, thereby affecting outdoor air quality, haze and smog, chronic health problems, damage to forests, ecosystems and global climate.

Burning of biomass and firewood will not stop, unless the government reaches power to villages under its programme of electricity for all, tentatively fixing timeline as 2020. The growth of electricity sector in India may help find a sustainable alternative to traditional fuel burning.

In the fiscal year 2014-15, electricity generated in utility sector was 1,030.785 billion KWh with a short fall of 38.138 billion KWh (−3.6%) against the anticipated 5.1% deficit. The peak load met was 141,180 MW with a short fall of requirement by 7,006 MW (−4.7%) against the 2.0% deficit anticipated.

In a May 2015 report, India's Central Electricity Authority anticipated, for the 2015–16 fiscal year, a base load energy deficit and peaking shortage to be 2.1% and 2.6% respectively. Southern and North Eastern regions are anticipated to face energy shortage up to 11.3%. The marginal deficit figures clearly reflect that India would become electricity surplus during the 12th five-year plan period.

Despite an ambitious rural electrification programme, some 400 million Indians, it is estimated, lose electricity access during blackouts. While 80% of the villages in India have at least an electricity line, but only 52.5% of rural households have access to electricity. In urban India, the access to electricity was 93.1% in 2008.

The overall electrification rate in India is 64.5% while 35.5% of the population still live without access to electricity.

According to a sample of 97,882 households made some time ago, electricity was the main source of lighting for 53% of rural households compared to 36% in 1993.

The 17th Electric Power Survey of India report claims:
- Over 2010–11, India's industrial demand accounted for 35% of electrical power requirement, domestic household use accounted for 28%, agriculture 21%, commercial 9%, public lighting and other miscellaneous applications accounted for the rest.
- The electrical energy demand for 2016–17 is expected to be at least 1,392 Tera Watt Hours, with a peak electric demand of 218 GW.
- The electrical energy demand for 2021–22 is expected to be at least 1,915 Tera Watt Hours, with a peak electric demand of 298 GW.

If current average transmission and distribution average losses remain same (32%), India needs to add about 135 GW of power generation capacity, before 2017, to satisfy the projected demand after losses.

McKinsey claims that India's demand for electricity may cross 300 GW, earlier than most estimates. To explain their estimates, they point to four reasons:
- If current average India's manufacturing sector is likely to grow faster than in the past.
- Domestic demand will increase more rapidly as the quality of life for more Indians improve.

- About 125,000 villages are likely to get connected to India's electricity grid.
- Blackouts and load shedding artificially suppresses demand; this demand will be sought as revenue potential by power distribution companies.

A demand of 300 GW will require about 400 GW of installed capacity, McKinsey notes.

The extra capacity is necessary to account for plant availability, infrastructure maintenance, spinning reserve and losses.

So, the challenges are enormous before the power sector. But the morass in the industry caused by gas pricing tussle between the government and private operators as also the coal de-allocation issue are also easing creating better atmosphere for renewed capacity addition at a faster pace than before.

Basically, India needs to substantially step up its energy generation to feed its growing manufacturing and other sectors through the conventional thermal and hydro sectors. The thermal sector has finite resources and increased demand also leads to coal imports at huge costs. Also, it has the attendant problem of throwing up particulate matter causing environmental pollution.

Carbon emissions are a major international issue under the ambit of climate change and control. Hydro sector is the answer as it's a renewable and clean energy but the difficult geographical terrain and security considerations puts tremendous constraints on its growth. Governments target of enhancing the capacity of non-conventional energy, solar and wind (including harassing the off shore wind energy) and biomass is ambitious with 175 GW target by 2022. It also throws up the potential challenges of grid integration, transmission and storage problems. For that huge investments are required in smart grids and integrated transmission net works. For this purpose a lot of private investment from both, the domestic and as well as the foreign required. India's twin strategy of relying alternatively on the non-conventional sources of energy could deliver additional energy. So India is increasing its footprint of nuclear power across India, kudankulam built with Russian technological help being one such example. India's aggressive foreign policy has led to assured nuclear fuel supplies from USA, France for its nuclear power plants. All in all, India is pursuing a comprehensive energy policy to sustain its energy security for the years to come.

Oil and Gas Sector – Status and Challenges

If the power sector in India sustains the growth of the manufacturing sector and other growth centres, the oil and gas virtually fuels the growth of the transport sector so vital for the economy to move things across vast spaces effectively and efficiently.

The Oil and Gas sector is one of the six core industries in India which is of strategic importance and plays a pivotal role in influencing decisions across other important spheres of the economy.

To recall one of government's effective strategies, In 1997–98, the New Exploration Licensing Policy (NELP) was envisioned to deal with the ever-growing gap between demand and supply of gas in India. A recent report indicates the oil and gas industry in India is anticipated to be valued over US$ 139,814.7 million by 2015. With India's economic growth closely linked to its energy demand, the need for oil and gas is projected to grow further, making it a fertile ground for investment.

To meet the growing demand, the Government of India has adopted several policies; including allowing 100 per cent foreign direct investment (FDI) in many segments of the sector, such as natural gas, petroleum products, and refineries, among others. The government's participation has made the oil and gas sector in the country a better target of investment. Today, it attracts both domestic and foreign investment, as attested by the presence of Reliance Industries Ltd. (RIL) and Cairn India.

Market Size

Backed by new oil fields, domestic oil output is anticipated to grow to 1 MBPD by FY16. With India developing gas-fired power stations, consumption is up more than 160 per cent since 1995. Gas consumption is likely to expand at a CAGR of 21 per cent during FY08-17.

Domestic production accounts for more than three-quarters of the country's total gas consumption. India has increasingly begun to rely on imported LNG; the country was the fifth-largest LNG importer in 2013, accounting for 5.5 per cent of global imports. India's LNG imports are forecast to increase at a CAGR of 33 per cent during 2012-17.

State-owned ONGC dominates the upstream segment (exploration and production), accounting for approximately 60 per cent of the country's total oil output (FY13).IOCL, which dominates the downstream sector, operates 11,214 km network of crude, gas and product pipelines, with a capacity of 1.6 MBPD of oil and 10 million metric standard cubic metre per day (MMSCMD) of gas. That's 30 per cent of the nation's total pipeline network. IOCL is the largest company, operating 10 out of 22 Indian refineries, with a combined capacity of 1.3 MBPD.

Investment

According to data released by the Department of Industrial Policy and Promotion (DIPP), the petroleum and natural gas sector attracted foreign direct investment (FDI) worth US$ 6,519.53 million between April 2000 and January 2015.

We can list the following as some of the major investments and developments in the oil and gas sector:

- Kirloskar Oil Engines Ltd. (KOEL) and MTU Friedrichshafen, GmbH have signed a memorandum of understanding (MoU). The MoU lays down exclusive cooperation on the building and commissioning of emergency diesel gensets (EDG).
- CDP Bharat Forge GmbH has acquired 100 per cent equity shares of Mécanique Générale Langroise (MGL) for • 11.8 million (US$ 12.91 million). The acquisition would consolidate Bharat Forge's position in the oil and gas sector by enhancing service offerings and geographical reach.
- Technip has won a • 100 million (US$ 109.37 million) contract from Oil and Natural Gas Corporation (ONGC) to build an onshore oil and gas terminal in Andhra Pradesh.
- Essar Oil Ltd has signed a deal with Russia-based OAO Rosneft to import 10 million tonnes (MT) of crude oil per year for 10 years.
- The oil marketing companies have reduced the price of non-subsidised liquefied petroleum cooking gas (LPG) by ₹ 43.5 (US$ 0.69) per cylinder. The companies have also reduced jet fuel rates by 12.5 per cent, the sixth straight reduction in prices since August 2014.
- Reliance Industries Ltd (RIL) and Mexican state-owned company Petroleos Mexicanos (Pemex) have entered

into a memorandum of understanding (MoU) for cooperation in the oil and gas sector.
- GAIL Global USA LNG LLC (GGULL) has signed an agreement with the US-based WGL Midstream Inc. for sourcing gas required to produce 2.5 MT of liquefied natural gas (LNG) a year at the Cove Point Terminal in Maryland, US.

Government Initiatives

Two landmark initiatives for energy efficiency – Design Guidelines for Energy Efficient Multi-Storey Residential Buildings and Star Ratings for Diesel Gensets and for Hospital Buildings – were launched by Dharmendra Pradhan, Minister of State with Independent Charge for Petroleum and Natural Gas, Government of India.

Some of the major initiatives taken by the Government of India to promote oil and gas sector are:
- India and Norway have discussed bilateral relationship between the two countries in the field of oil and natural gas and decided to extend cooperation in hydrocarbon exploration.
- To strengthen the country's energy security, oil diplomacy initiatives have been intensified through meaningful engagements with hydrocarbon rich countries.
- PAHAL – Direct Benefit Transfer for LPG consumer (DBTL) scheme launched in 54 districts on November 11, 2014 and expanded to rest of the country on January 1, 2015 will cover 15.3 crore active LPG consumers of the country.
- 24 x 7 LPG service via web launched to provide LPG consumers an integrated solution to carry out all

- Special dispensation for North East Region: For incentivising exploration and production in North East Region, 40 per cent subsidy on gas price has been extended to private companies operating in the region, along with ONGC and OIL.
- The Cabinet Committee on Economic Affairs (CCEA), chaired by Prime Minister Mr. Narendra Modi, has approved a mechanism for procurement of Ethanol by Public Sector Oil Marketing Companies (OMCs) to carry out the Ethanol Blended Petrol (EBP) Program.

Road Ahead

By 2015-16, India's demand for gas is set to touch 124 MTPA against a domestic supply of 33 MTPA and higher imports of 47.2 MTPA, leaving a shortage of 44 MTPA, as per projections by the Petroleum and Natural Gas Ministry of India. Moreover, Business Monitor International (BMI) predicts that India will account for 12.4 per cent of Asia-Pacific regional oil demand by 2015.

Challenges and Opportunities

The greatest challenge the Oil and Gas sector faces today is how to meet the growing demand for fuels by the transportation sector by producing crude from ageing oil fields and mounting refining costs. The Bombay High, the work horse for domestic crude production by state owned ONGC, is nearing its 50 year life cycle of productivity, meaning that its peak production is over and now production will only dwindle.

The option is now to go for deep sea drilling in the same offshore area which requires enormous costs of equipment to be deployed, nearly four to five times of what India today spends on drilling exploration and production activities.

One of the strategies government adopted to overcome the problem of reduced supplies from aging fields was to acquire oil assets abroad. India has added oil assets in Russia and Vietnam where it has set up rigs to explore and produce oil for exports. This strategy has substantially added to the energy security of the country and India is now looking at assets in West Africa where new oilfields have been discovered and the regimes there have sought Indian help which comes at competitive rates such as in Mozambique.

The challenge the refining sector faces today is to increase capacity and to adopt newer technologies to produce green fuels.

They have to be in tune with the latest generation Euro standards of cleanliness in both diesel and petrol, the main fuels used in the transportation sector besides aviation turbine fuel used in the civil aviation sector by aircraft.

The opportunity for the refining sector is in terms of falling international prices of crude. Brent crude which is the standard reference price for India to import crude oil from mostly the gulf countries has slid to a remarkable US$ 49 per barrel, which is about slightly more than half the price of crude when it reached a peak of US$ 100 per barrel inflating India's oil import bill. India which was bleeding some years ago gets an unexpected bonus in terms of saving valuable foreign exchange in reduced cost of importing crude and petroleum products which can be recycled for the growth of the country's petroleum sector. Its estimated that billions of USD are being saved due to the fall in international prices of crude which is likely to stay.

Why? Because oil prices which are controlled by the cartel OPEC comprising mostly gulf countries has been faced with an extraordinary situation of an unprecedented glut in oil supplies, meaning for the first time Oil supply outstrips demand worldwide. Recession is one of the factors which is inducing slower growth in many countries. Secondly, USA which was the biggest consumer of the OPEC oil supplies indulged in a tremendous cut back on its demand as it started relying more on its internal oil and gas supplies by exploiting its huge reserves of shale oil and gas.

OPEC had errant members who did not adhere to their production cutbacks to keep prices stable and high which resulted in a glut as demand tapered globally and led to a huge stockpile of crude not being exported.

After having discussed scenario in Power and Oil and Gas sector; lets now analyse how the infrastructure sector is going to move forward.

There can be no doubt about the necessity of creating infrastructure which cannot happen without participation of private sector. Infrastructure is basic requirement as well as force multiplier which is required for growth of the country. All this cannot happen without creating an enabling environment for participation of private sector. This requirement is based on the fact that by a rough estimate there is a gap of at least 5 trillion rupees for infrastructure which can only come from private sector. We must also be aware of the fact that spending on infrastructure grew only from 2003, from 4.1% to 7.2% in 2012. Government spending can also be increased on infrastructure but for that there has to be a drastic cut down on wasteful Government expenditure such as subsidies etc. and by meeting tax collection targets through reforms in the taxation structure. Even then this cannot be any substitute for private sector participation.

There are some truths which have been learnt the hard way in the last few decades by the country. These are; the delays in land acquisition led to huge cost overruns; delay in regulatory clearances/failure of bidding procedures/judicial intervention (right or wrong)/irresponsible functioning by banks/ Government not delivering on many fronts – all these lead to virtual stopping of private sector participation in creating infrastructure. Taking the example of power sector, which is in a mess now, a large capacity has gone off the block because of de-allocation of coal blocks, another large capacity got derailed because of coal linkage problems and no gas being available. There will be huge cost to pay by the public sector banks if these projects are not sorted out because banks will have approximately ₹ 60,000 crore of nonperforming assets in this sector. There is huge opportunity cost involved here. This is just one example. There are many other sectors like roads, ports, civil aviation, telecom, which all need infrastructure creation on most immediate basis.

The challenges for enhancing infrastructure creation are of many types but mainly in the area of untimely decisions in respect of tariffs and compensation by regulators. There are transfer pricing problems which need to be resolved. There is controversy in the land acquisition act which needs immediate sorting out without making political mincemeat of it. The National Highway Authority of India needs to gear up its resolution mechanism to provide time-bound decisions.

Government approvals and their reliability are a matter of concern for foreign investors if they are going to be challenged in future or set aside by the regulators or judicial authorities. **Retrospective Taxation and unfair labor laws are also issues of great concern to foreign investors which only**

goes in the long run to create an atmosphere of distrust leading to discouraging them to consider India as an investment destination. There is a huge lack of depth in hedging instruments in currency markets.

If this situation prevails, the role of private sector participation in future will be called into question.

Every time Government tries to disinvest in a public sector unit, only the state run insurers or public sector banks come to its rescue and buy the shares most of the time. This could lead to a stressful financial situation in future. The cases like 2G Spectrum, coal blocks deallocation Vodafone/nokia case, shut down of iron ore mines by judicial intervention, Niyamgiri Boxide Mines of Orissa, all these are disincentives and we need to think hard about it. The problem is compounded by the frequent power cuts/poor roads/congested airports and railways etc.

There is an immediate need for irreversible time bound govt. approvals and clearances. We also need to relax or modify the acquisition process for creation of infrastructure. The government should provide clarity on tax laws. There is a need for timely allocation of mines. There is need to involve State Governments in policy-making. In the case of power sector, there is a need for capacity-building of the regulators and time-bound tariff approvals.

In the case of the telecom sector, there is need for a long term policy and a road map and there is a need for proper valuation of the spectrum secured by the operators by financial institutions for funding the bidding process.

In the case of road projects there is a need for shaping of all proceeds with the States without which their involvement will be minimal. There is a need for huge effort in exploiting renewable energy technologies. **India has a 7600 KM long coast line from which wind energy can be harnessed.** The solar potential is least exploited in India. The traditional Indian Power Sector also needs creation of infrastructure for power evacuation. There is need for ensuring supply of fuels like coal and gas to the power plants after addressing the challenge of fuel transport. There is a urgent need for corporatizing state level electricity boards and other authorities.

Last but not the least, there is need for investor protection and credit availability in India. The contracts should be simple and enforceable. There should be a certainty and continuity in the Govt. policy. There is need for huge private sector participation in Railways/municipalities/water management/waste disposal but for that there is need for giving them a good revenue model without which they will not be attracted and there is no denying the fact that huge capacity building for man power in this sector is required.

The ongoing plan had envisaged an investment of '30 lakh crore in infrastructure creation, 40% coming from private sector investment. Whatever investment that has come from the private sector is nothing but peanuts. Does private sector have the capacity to raise this money? They have taken huge loans from the banks causing serious concern about the health of public sector banks, because of rising incidence of gross NPAs.

Dilution of equity is also not a solution for them. A foreign direct investment is negligible. The yield of these projects is not very attractive. Unless and until the private sector is given protected revenue, the costs of their capital will remain high because of risk premium being high. How can we then have a huge private sector investment?

Dispute resolution and arbitration also calls for huge capacity development in this area. Instead of tariffs being decided by the regulator, why cannot they be market driven? It is a sad truth that we do not have very capable Administrators who can apprehend risks involved in a project and then structure the agreements accordingly. Rather there is an emphasis on putting more and more clauses for saving everybody's assets in case of a failure. This mindset has to be changed.

We have been talking of private-public partnership in a very loud volume but how much of it has gone in actual creation of infrastructure needs to be seen and we must remember that PPP is not a panacea for everything. As it is, all over the world, it has been a mixed bag – succeeded somewhere and failed elsewhere. It is to be accepted by the Government that although we may talk very big about the private sector participation in creation of infrastructure, still it is going to be by and large the Government's responsibility because even the private sector in India has the constraint for its financial capacity and the ability to raise resources. And there is no doubt that if the Government has good expertise to develop good concession agreements and good revenue models for the private sector and there are positive regulators and arbitrators, the investment climate will be better and infrastructure creation will become a reality instead of being a pipedream.

Having said this, if infrastructure has to grow faster, it is obvious that both the public sector comprising state owned enterprises and the private sector consisting of Indian and foreign enterprises need to pool their resources together tapping external finance to fund the infrastructure growth which is going to such huge amounts of investments. So one of the successful models tried out globally is the public private partnership which we analyse in the next few pages.

❑

PUBLIC-PRIVATE PARTNERSHIP

A World Bank report says that India is second only to China in terms of the number of Public Private Partnership (PPP) projects. During the 12th Five-Year Plan (2012-17), the target is to achieve 47 per cent of total infrastructure investments through private funding, up from 25 per cent in the 10th Five-Year Plan.

The ongoing Five Year Plan (2012-2017) has an ambitious target of infrastructure investment which is envisaged at US $ 1 trillion. The projected investment is double the investment proposed in the XI Plan and 27 per cent of the gross domestic savings.

As the task of funding is enormous, with limited availability of public resources for investment in physical infrastructure, it is necessary to look at how to increase investment in infrastructure through a combination of public investment, Public Private Partnerships (PPPs) and occasionally, exclusive private investment wherever feasible.

Needless to say that the use of PPP an as instrument of procurement for creation of infrastructure assets and delivery of public services has been recognized globally. Apart from bridging the deficit in financing of public projects, PPPs also helps to bring in new and cost effective technology for creation of infrastructure assets, managerial efficiency, competency for operation and maintenance of the created assets and the contractual accountability on the private party to ensure timely and quality infrastructure service to the end users.

As a result, private investment in infrastructure has picked up in recent years, encouraging the government to go for a more ambitious infrastructure creation drive through greater emphasis on PPP mode of execution. The private sector is expected to contribute at least half of the over $1 trillion dollar investment planned in infrastructure in the XII plan (2012-17), Government Initiatives for promoting PPPs.

The Public Private Partnership (PPP) Cell under the Finance Ministry is tasked with the responsibility for matters pertaining to Public Private Partnerships, including policy, schemes, programmes and capacity building and all other matters relating to mainstreaming PPPs. Principal Functions of the Cell:

- Matters and proposals relating to clearance by Public Private Partnership Appraisal Committee (PPPAC).
- Matters and proposals relating to the Scheme for Financial Support to Public Private Partnerships in Infrastructure-Viability Gap Funding (VGF) Scheme.
- Matters and proposals relating to the Scheme for India Infrastructure Project Development Fund.
- Policy matters related to Public Private Partnerships (including Model Concession Agreement).
- Developing multi-pronged and innovative interventions and support mechanisms for facilitating PPPs in the country, including Technical Assistance programmes from bilateral and multilateral agencies on mainstreaming PPPs and support to State and local governments.
- Managing training programmes, strategies, exposures for capacity building for PPPs.

- Subject of advocacy for greater acceptability towards PPPs Institution building for mainstreaming PPPs.
- Matters relating to management of PPP related information, including www.pppinindia.com and www.InfrastructureIndia.gov.in.
- The Toolkit for the use by PPP practitioners across India in both the public and private sectors, http://toolkit.pppinindia.com.
- Other policy/Parliament related matters concerning PPPs. The Government of India is actively encouraging PPPs through several initiatives. The appraisal mechanism for the PPP projects has been streamlined to ensure speedy appraisal of projects, eliminate delays, adopt international best practices and have uniformity in appraisal mechanism and guidelines. The appraisal mechanism notified includes setting up of the Public Private Partnership Appraisal Committee (PPPAC) responsible for the appraisal of PPP projects in the Central Sector.

Standardized bidding and contractual documents have been notified. These include model Request for Qualification (RFQ); Request for Proposal (RFP) and RFP for technical consultants; Model Concession Agreements (MCAs) for different sectors including Highways (both National and State Highways), Ports, Urban Transport (Metro), Power sectors and Manuals of Standards and Specifications have been developed and standardized. Further, Project Sponsors are encouraged to award projects through a transparent open competitive bidding process, which leads to greater transparency and consistency to the bid process and terms of contract.

The Government has created a Viability Gap Funding Scheme for PPP projects. Infrastructure projects are often not commercially viable on account of having substantial sunk investment and low returns. However, they continue to be economically essential. Accordingly, the Viability Gap Funding Scheme has been formulated which provides financial support in the form of grants, one time or deferred, to infrastructure projects undertaken through public private partnerships with a view to make them commercially viable. The Scheme provides total Viability Gap Funding up to twenty percent of the total project. The Government or statutory entity that owns the project may, if it so decides, provides additional grants out of its budget up to further twenty percent of the total project cost. Viability Gap Funding under the Scheme is normally in the form of a capital grant at the stage of project construction.

The Government has also set up India Infrastructure Finance Company Limited (IIFCL) with the specific mandate to play a catalytic role in the Infrastructure sector by providing long-term debt for financing infrastructure projects. IIFCL funds viable infrastructure projects through Long Term Debt, Refinance to Banks and Financial Institutions for loans granted by them, with tenor exceeding 10 years or any other mode approved by the Government.

The Indian government has planned to build 100 smart cities. The government has allocated US$ 1.2 billion for this project in its 2014-15 budget. This plan would need more PPP's for better and fast execution.

Looking back, since the last one decade, there has been a lot of talk about Public Private Partnership (PPP) which is an agreement between the government and Private Sector for the purpose of provisioning of infrastructure for the purpose of provisioning of infrastructure or public services of any kind. The idea of PPP was to bring the best of the both sectors for accomplishing the objective of speedy development of infrastructure without which no further growth can happen in no further growth can happen in any country. As we have discussed it earlier in one of the chapters that the amount of funds required for infrastructure development are far too high and government alone cannot provide these funds. This has to happen by harnessing private sector investment and seek their operational efficiency for providing public assets and services.

Since 2007, Government of India has acknowledged the role to be played by PPP and a policy was evolved based on which the Department of Economic Affairs, Ministry of Finance started creating the data base of PPP projects in the country. This data base in 2011 showed that almost 750 PPP projects had been awarded or were under progress either at the operational stage or implementation. Most of these projects were in bridges and road sector but now the PPP in other sectors is also growing. Andhra Pradesh and Madhya Pradesh have been the leading States in terms of number and value of PPP Projects. At the National level, NHAI has successfully used the PPP model. There have been various forms of PPP models in India but the most preferred one has been in our ownership of under lying assets remains with the public entity. There has been key model, BOT model and performance based management or maintains contracts. Some projects were also contracted on BOO model but it has not been a very successful mode. A massive effort has gone in the preparation of PPP tool kit to improve position making process and establish all model bidding documents and understanding financial support through viability gap funding and a mechanism for appropriate public oversight and monitoring all these projects.

The PPP projects cannot succeed without creating an enabling environment which includes a viability gap funding, long tenure lending and refinancing facility, creating infrastructure debt funds and providing policy support to appropriate credit structures. It also requires capacity building interventions for creating a profession which provide competencies and technical support for these projects.

It is not that the creation of PPP mode has solved all the problems. First of all just 5 States account for 60% of the total PPP projects in the country which means most of the States have not taken up this route. Only sectors like roads/ports/airports have been cove red under the ambit of PPP. The most successful projects in the country under PPP have been hi-tech city, international airport, Krishnapattinam port etc. in Andhra Pradesh. Even Bangalore International Airport, Dahej L&G terminal etc. have good examples of successful PPP. But there are lots of challenges for PPP in India. For example, there is no independent regulator, the database does not exist online and there is limited capacity to undertake complex projects. It is neither available at the Central Govt. level nor at State level. The concession authorities do not have a very good idea about doing a proper feasible study giving fast clearances and development at mutually attractive concession terms.

But the international examples of U.K., Australia, Brazil/Philippines etc. show that PPP can be a big boost for developing infrastructure in a speedy manner. As we have discussed earlier there is need for using PPP in Railways, higher education, power, urban infrastructure and health sector.

PPP can be boosted by creating an independent institutional structure for handling PPP data base, best practices and model documents. There is need for developing separate sector specific regulators and also to create a system for dissemination of information of PPP. The government also needs to undertake capacity building measures at the Central/State/Municipal levels. There is also need to hire consultations of the highest quality consultants instead of just hiring people who charge the lowest fees. There is also a need for effective and optional allocation of risks/authority/accountability between public and private sector. Furthermore there is need for the Government to develop a corporate bond market and encourage participation of pension funds from the insurance companies for investment in infrastructure. The Government needs to introduce measures which will bring global and domestic private equity funds into infrastructure sector. There is also a need for developing hedging mechanism for external borrowings and investments so that companies can protect themselves. Without all these measures, it will not be possible to unleash the true potential of PPP in development of infrastructure. PPP all for that matter in changes in Indian governance cannot happen without the government managing its civil services or bureaucracy in a better manner. This is feasible from the fact that despite the present government's Will to reform India ineffectiveness of the bureaucracy is holding it back. The intentions are not getting converted into outcomes. There is need for empowering the bureaucracy while at the same time ensuring accountability. But a high degree of scrutiny and micro management can be counter predicted. It can cause paralysis of decision making because then the safety factor becomes more important than being dynamic. Too much concentration of power at any one centre in the Government can also not be very conducive. Giving reasonable time frames for performance or achievement is also essential. Uncertainty of tenure as well as the fear caused by RTI have caused several services to be... to take any indulgence. The subjectivity of appraisal process also does not held it. A word of mouth appraisal about personal attributions have to be more important than work outcome, we shall not reach anywhere. Probably, there is also need for induction of subject matter specialist at some places which should be clearly defined.

Having spoken about the Economy and infrastructure sector that needs to engineer growth with particular focus on the power and oil and gas sector and the need for taking PPP route to raise funds for the same, its now time to look at the status of the agriculture sector which was primarily the focus for growth immediately after India attained independence. The sector has seen growth but not substantial as other sectors of the economy. The average 4 per cent growth is considered by many as tardy. But the cycle of droughts and floods and the inability to store the buffer stock of foodgrains in an efficient manner have been some of the major problems facing this sector.

❑

INDIAN AGRICULTURE

If one were to trace the history of Indian agriculture it actually dates back to the Rigveda. India actually ranks 2nd worldwide in its farm output. Official statistics show that agriculture and allied sectors like forestry and fisheries accounted for 13.7% of the GDP (Gross Domestic Product) in 2013 with about 50% of the total workforce of the country working in this sector. It's disheartening to note that, agriculture which was the mainstay of the country soon after independence, its economic contribution to India's GDP is steadily declining with the country's overall economic growth. And yet, agriculture is demographically the broadest economic sector in India and still plays a significant role in the overall socio-economic fabric of the country.

The Rome based Food and Agriculture Organisaton (FAO) under the auspices of the United Nations (UN) claims that India is the world's largest producer of many fresh fruits and vegetables, milk, major spices, select fibrous crops such as jute, several staples such as millets and castor oil seed.

India is also the second largest producer of wheat and rice, the world's major food staples. India is also the world's second or third largest producer of several dry fruits, agriculture-based textile raw materials, roots and tuber crops, pulses, farmed fish, eggs, coconut, sugarcane and umerous vegetables.

India is ranked among the top five countries of the world producers of over 80% of agricultural produce items, including many cash crops such as coffee and cotton. India is also one of the world's five largest producers of livestock and poultry meat, with one of the fastest growth rates.

According to some claims, India's population is growing faster than its ability to produce rice and wheat. Other recent studies claim India can easily feed its growing population, plus produce wheat and rice for global exports, if it can reduce food staple spoilage, improve its infrastructure and raise its farm productivity to those achieved by other developing countries such as Brazil and China.

2011 goes down in Indian history as one when an all time high record production of 85.9 million tonnes of wheat was achieved which was a 6.4% increase from a year earlier. Rice output in India also hit a new record at 95.3 million tonnes, a 7% increase from the year earlier. Lentils and many other food staples production also increased year over year. Indian farmers thus produced about 71 kilograms of wheat and 80 kilograms of rice for every member of Indian population in 2011. The per capita supply of rice every year in India is now higher than the per capita consumption of rice every year in Japan.

India exported US$ 39 billion worth of agricultural products in 2013, making it the seventh largest agricultural exporter worldwide, and the sixth largest net exporter. Its net exports have grown from about $ 5 billion in 2003, to a net value that was double than agriculture exports of combined European Union (EU-28), making it the fastest growing exporter of agricultural products over a 10 year period, with an average annual export value growing at 21%.

It has become one of the world's largest supplier of rice, cotton, sugar and wheat. India exported around 2 million metric tonnes of wheat and 2.1 million metric tonnes of rice in 2011 to Africa, Nepal, Bangladesh and other regions around the world. Aquaculture and catch fishery is amongst the fastest growing industries in India. Between 1990 and 2010, Indian fish capture harvest doubled, while aquaculture harvest tripled. In 2008, India was the world's sixth largest producer of marine and freshwater capture fisheries, and the second largest aquaculture farmed fish producer. **India exported 600,000 metric tonnes of fish products to nearly half of all the world's countries.**

India has shown a steady average nationwide annual increase in the kilograms produced per hectare for various agricultural items, over the last 60 years. These gains have come mainly from India's Green Revolution, improving road and power generation infrastructure, knowledge of gains and reforms. Despite these recent accomplishments, agriculture in India has the potential for major productivity and total output gains, because crop yields in India are still just 30% to 60% of the best sustainable crop yields achievable in the farms of developed as well as other developing countries. Additionally, losses after harvest due to poor infrastructure and unorganised retail cause India to experience some of the highest food losses in the world.

There are few facts about Indian Agriculture which merit our attention. India has nearly one tenth of world's arable land and at least one fifth of world's irrigated land. It has excellent resources and well diversified climate because of which it has potential to become the world's largest food factory. Also India ranks number one in production of milk, pulses, sugar, banana, guava and mangoes and ranks number two in rice, wheat vegetables and many other horticulture products. But it is also a sad truth that post harvesting losses are huge; between 25 to 40% of total production across all value chains amounting to billions of dollars per annum. It is ironical that these losses are mainly due to lack of scientific management and good storage facilities at right locations. It is a happy augury that policy making bodies, government departments and the private sector are now looking at the creation of vast network of cold chains and high quality storage bins so that post harvesting losses are avoided. Perishables like vegetables can be preserved through cold chains and cereals such as rice, wheat can be scientifically stored in stainless steel bins. Few more facts need to be noted. Per hectare yield of cereals in India is much poorer as compared to China or Vietnam or even Bangladesh. China and Vietnam harness average 5 tonne per hectare of foodgrains as compared to India's 2.5 tonnes per hectare. Our water usage is one of the worst. We have a huge burden of subsidies. We are not at all serious about exploring potential of genetically modified crops suited to our conditions. We have done nothing in last three decades to incentivize private sector investment in agriculture which is hampered because of obsolete laws concerning land lease/contract farming/APMCs. We have hardly any agricultural marketing infrastructure except few successful experiments in some states.

Our requirement of food is going to be very high because our population from 1.25 billion today is likely to surpass China by 2050. Our population's average age is going to be much lower, meaning bulk of the population is going to be in the younger generation, leading to more consumption. Furthermore we will have a very fast urbanization in next 15 years which will put lot of pressure on scarce resources like land, water and energy. Furthermore, our average per capita income will rise substantially leading to much higher consumption demand. So question before us is whether we will be able to grow sufficiently to feed our own people? The answer is not very simple. Assuming that production and productivity of main cereals like rice and wheat continues at present pace, we should have no problem in meeting our requirement at least till 2030. But beyond that it may be difficult to estimate.

There are further challenges which need to be taken into account. There is continuous depletion of ground water in most areas where intensive cropping has been done. Water conservations judicious use of scarce water resources is the most urgent need of India's agriculture sector. The scientific methods of irrigation like drip irrigation and providing only the required amount of water to the crop must be followed extensively. Learning from Israel's experimentations should be made use of in cropping and harvesting. Because of continuously rising cost of inputs, farming alone is becoming non-remunerative for farmers and without subsidies farmers will not survive. But subsidies are unsustainable. Although they give faster political returns, in the longer run if agriculture has to grow, we need more investment in this sector than subsidization. The returns from investment will be four times more than the subsidy route which we are using at present.

Another challenge is from climate change. The temperatures are rising everywhere which are going to hit crops like wheat badly. There is more and more likelihood of extreme climatic events leading to more floods and droughts. We need to streamline our policies to use water more rationally. The best solution could probably lie in our often discussed national river linking project which can be a great force multiplier. We can improve water use in existing 60 million hectare irrigated land and cause our productivity to jump many times.

There is need to revamp the laws for permitting land lease/contract farming and abolition of APMCs so that private sector investment can come in agriculture.

We also need to remember that this will be required even for the next growth cycle of value addition by high value non-farm products like horticulture, dairy, fisheries etc. We also need to think about agriculture marketing infrastructure which now need to be improved on country-wide scale instead of just having some successful examples in Andhra Pradesh or Gujarat or Maharashtra. We need to create a unified online marketing network just as it has been done to some extent in Karnataka so that we capture the details of farmers and their produce. For getting the best prices to farmers we need to facilitate online bidding by buyers from anywhere in the world. This will also require creation of infrastructure like cold chains and storage facilities. We also need to ensure that benefits of value addition go to farmers themselves. Unless and until farming becomes remunerative, there is no chance of growth in agriculture in future.

This is also the truth that future of farming is not in farming alone but in food processing for which we need to create value chains all across. There are huge business opportunities for India in dairy produce/meat/fisheries/horticulture products/cotton/rice. Agricultural growth depends on proper incentivisation and innovations. We need to look seriously at potential of GM crops. If we do not want seeds from outside because of health concerns, in that case we can upgrade our own research and develop activity and develop our own GM seeds from Indian gene pools suited to our climatic conditions. But we should not keep shying away from this responsibility.

It may also be kept in mind that although the global food prices at present are stable but all over the world, investments in agriculture sector have not been very high because of which world production of foodgrains remains stagnant and one or two years of worldwide droughts or bad climatic conditions can cause huge volatility in food prices like what happened in 2008-09 and subsequent years. There is every reason for India to take all steps as listed above to increase its production and productivity (not only of rice and wheat but also of other crops). There will be always a rising demand all over the world for food grains so any excess quantity can always be exported at a very good price.

The question of food security for domestic masses is also related to food grains production. Food security depends upon on many factors like availability, economic access, absorption capacity and stability of food systems. This effectively means that domestic production has to be high and food inflation to be low. It is important not only to provide quantity of food grains like rice and wheat but also to ensure good nutrition to all in the country. For stability of food system; there has to be sufficient buffer stocks and trade of food grains in good health to ensure availability to all at affordable prices. It is a debatable point whether the current targeted public distribution system has done its job or not? Whether it needs to be totally replaced by the direct cash transfers to poor population so that they can buy their food grains? There are some states like Tamil Nadu who have done a universal public distribution system and exhort its virtues.

But one thing is clear that direct cash transfers can certainly bring down leakage of PDS to almost minimal level. Therefore, time may have come to experiment with direct cash transfers or food coupons at same places and see how successful it is? But whether market forces will keep food prices at affordable rates will only be known after same year's experience.

Food Inflation: Besides there is the issue of inflation in India which is peculiar in sense that food is a major part of the Consumer Price Index (CPI). Food is not a market. Some Government departments try to provide due to which supply side becomes non-responsive. This is what is often referred to as the supply side constraint.

Till an industrial food market emerges without inter-state barriers, India will remain trapped in this kind of inflation where price signals do not work quickly and effectively. This is another reason for coming up with a policy frame work which creates natural food market and helps us deal with our inflation which is more or less directly proportional to the volatility in food prices and Government controls a large chunk of major food grains because of its massive PDS commitment.

There has been a huge effort by Government of India and State Governments to do end to end computerization of TPDS operations. More than 13 states have completed digitization of ration cards. States like Chhattisgarh, Delhi and Karnataka have computerized the entire supply chain management. Most states have set up transparency portals and many have set up a Grievance Redressal mechanism but how far these will ensure doorstep delivery of food grains to consumers remains to be seen. Besides there is also the challenge of weaknesses of private trade in a very large public distribution system. There is also the real danger of recycling of food grains. This dependence on wheat/rice bank, PDS is also leading to no diversification of agriculture. There is no doubt about the fact that primarily income policy should be used to equity objective and price policy for efficient allocation of resources and growth. Although one cannot conclusively say whether the private markets are the best mechanism for handling of grains but as far as possible, they should be allowed to do so for efficiency and correct price discovery.

There is need for developing India as an international destination for processed foods just like it has been done in Thailand and some other countries where they have marketing hubs for various commodities. The idea for creating such hubs is that they are near the growing areas with easy transportation facility. Also the value addition happens at the point of production itself and it leads to a better price payment to farmers. These hubs shall have facilities for international buyers and are connected to the international markets. If this is done at around 50 places in the country; India as an exporter of value added horticulture products shall be established in the world markets.

Furthermore, there is need for biologizing the economy for green growth so that alternatives to fossil fuels shall be developed for mitigating danger of climate change.

Bio-economy not only refers to greening of economy but it goes beyond agriculture/forestry and food processing to chemical/pharmaceuticals/textiles and manufacturing activities in various sectors. The idea is based on innovations like bio based construction materials, various types of bio energies etc. This is an absolutely new area. There is a need to undertake massive research here. The reasons are not very far to seek. We also cannot deny the fact that approximately 400 million tonnes of cattle dung is used for cooking fuel, which could be used as manure. We could have also used huge surplus of forest residues for fuel production which we are not able to do. There is also case for bio fortification meaning production of new 'micro nutrient – rich crops' in the country. And in case we are talking of food security for all, then we will never be able to ensure it just by traditional methods. We will have to make enhanced investments in science and technology, GM Crops, new types of foods so that security both in terms of quantity and quality (nutrition) can be ensured.

Having said all what was necessary about Indian economy, infrastructure, PPP and agriculture sector, we need to have a book at Indian urbanisation because *without* having real good smart cities; India can't hope to become a great power.

❑

INDIAN URBANISATION

India's urbanisation is said to have begun soon after independence, as the country adopted a mixed economy, giving rise to the development of the private sector. Urbanisation in India is now taking place at a faster rate than was imagined. The population residing in urban areas in India, according to 1901 census, was just 11.4%. This however increased to 28.53% according to 2001 census, and crossing 30% as per 2011 census, standing at 31.16%. According to a survey by UN State of the World Population report in 2007, by 2030, 40.76% of country's population is expected to reside in urban areas. As per World Bank, India, along with China, Indonesia, Nigeria, and the United States, will lead the world's urban population surge by 2050.

Mumbai saw large-scale rural-urban migration in the 21st century. Mumbai accommodates 12.5 million people, and is the largest metropolis by population in India, followed by Delhi with 11 million inhabitants. Witnessing the fastest rate of urbanisation in the world, as per 2011 census, Delhi's population rose by 4.1%, Mumbai's by 3.1% and Kolkata's by 2% as per 2011 census compared to 2001 census.

Maharashtra was the most urbanized state in India till 1991, stood behind Tamil Nadu in 2001 and third after it in 2011, with Kerala being second, with the urban-total state population ratio. However, Maharashtra's urban population of 41 million, far exceeds that of Tamil Nadu which is at 27 million, as per the 2001 census. Rapid rise in urban population, in India, is leading to many problems like increasing slums, decrease in standard of living in urban areas, also causing environmental damage.

India has around 300 million people living in metropolitan areas. This has greatly caused slum problems, with so many people over crowding cities and forcing people to live in unsafe conditions which also includes illegal buildings. Water lines, roads and electricity are lacking which is causing fall of living standards. It is also adding to the problem of all types of pollution.

Urbanization also results in a disparity in the market, owing to the large demands of the growing population and the primary sector struggling to cope with them.

Viewed against this background, India needs urbanization very badly and that too very fast. A flip side to this is that, however enchanted we may be with our romantic vision of life in the villages, there are just not enough jobs there. The Gandhian scale of industries at village level is no longer viable because economies of scale are rising. Migration of populations from the rural to urban areas has become an inevitable necessity. Although it is not forced, it's rather an adaptive response of the people. The only need of the hour is that people need to be taught useful skills for purposeful employment in towns or growth centers near the villages. The best jobs will come from rural tourism natural resource management, urban and informal sector and industrial non-farm sector. Livelihood creation has to be fostered by households themselves instead of Government doing it.

But Government has to provide enabling conditions for households so as to maximize livelihood creation. Without adding approximately 1.5 crore new livelihoods per annum we cannot bring unemployment down. Economy is already generating 90 lakh livelihoods per annum. So, we need to add another 60 lakhs per annum. The best option would be for people to live in villages and commute to nearby towns to earn their livelihood, but for that also infrastructure and amenities in villages will have to be up-scaled considerably.

The fact of the matter is that rural livelihoods are becoming redundant. Indian cities at present are polluted, congested, over crowded with meager infrastructure and unmanageable traffic. We will need to transform our cities very fast. Let's not be dismayed by this because this is nothing new happening to us. The same thing happened in U.K., France and rest of Europe also several years ago. In the transition stage they were as bad as Indian cities and later got better infrastructure and they have become what they are today, modern cities replete with facilities for the population. We need to keep in mind that urbanization is a long gestation activity. It does not happen overnight. So we need to plan accordingly. The most important component of a 'city' planning anywhere is efficiently managing the mobility of people between their homes and work places and markets. There can be different models for planning this but unfortunately in India, city planning does not work because our approach and tools both seem wrong.

We are using a central planning approach with license raj for most activities with no participation from the citizens and consumer bodies. The challenges of urbanization at present in India are widening of streets, providing space for pedestrians to walk, providing roads/parks/amenities like water supply/

drainage, etc. There are other challenges like managing the peripheral growth, housing for poor and regularization of illegal colonies etc.

The land transformation methods have also to be standardized for fast development. There are various methods like Laissez Faire approach, combining development planning with Laissez Faire or acquiring land and developing it. We can allow private townships to come up with infrastructure alone to be developed by the Government. There can be another method called 'DPTP' which means a development plan followed by town planning. In this there are no acquisitions involved. It is almost like 'land pooling'. This has been done successfully in Ahmedabad and can be explored for other towns and cities. This is more participatory in nature and cuts down the delays. There is also need for a professional breed of training of city managers and municipal administrators for the purpose of an urgent service delivery. Future cities/towns would require such managers to sustain growth and private delivery of services. **Some rough estimates say that at least ₹ 40 lakh crores (@ 2009-10 prices) will be required for urban growth in India. So without private sector investments coming in and innovative methods of funding; it will be impossible to do it.**

It has also to be realized that State Governments will have to do capacity building and awareness creation because it is their job and without their cooperation and help, Central Government will not be able to do it.

After having dealt with economy, infrastructure, agriculture and need for cities, Our nation cannot claim to see great heights unless and until it... has a very good health infrastructure and system for all its citizens. Let's have a look at our health sector.

❑

HEALTH SECTOR

Under the Indian constitution, health is a state subject. This means every state becomes responsible for "raising the level of nutrition and the standard of living of its people and it becomes its primary duty to improve public health. The National Health Policy was endorsed by the Parliament of India in 1983 and updated in 2002. The National Health Policy is now being worked further in 2015 and a draft for public consultation has been released.

The private health sector is the dominant healthcare provider in both urban and rural Indian households as per nationwide surveys.

The ongoing five-year plan has taken a look at health care in the country based on the recommendation of a High Level Experts Group (HLEG) and other stakeholder consultations. The long term objective of this strategy is to establish a system of Universal Health Coverage (UHC) in the country.

The High-Level Expert Group report has recommended an increase in public expenditure on health from 1.58 per cent of GDP as at present to 2.1 per cent of GDP by the end of 12th five-year plan. It is still much lower than the global median of 5 per cent. One of the biggest problems facing health care in India is that, inadequately funded public health services has pushed a sizeable population to incur heavy out of pocket expenditure on services accessed from the private sector. Even in public sector hospitals, out of pocket expenditure is on the rise, since lack of medicines at public health care facilities forces patients to buy them from outside. Often, resulting in a very high financial burden on families in case of severe illnesses.

Even though, the 12th plan document has expressed concern over high out-of-pocket (OOP) expenditure, it has not specified any target or time frame for reducing this expense. Its opined by experts that OOP can be reduced only by increasing public expenditure on health and by setting up widespread public health service providers. However, the planning commission, now renamed as Niti Ayog, is planning to do this by regulating private health care providers. It is apparent that the commission or Ayog take comfort from the fact the HLEG report which admits that, 'the transformation of India's health system to become an effective platform for UHC is an evolutionary process that will span several years'.

The seemingly controversial point is that Instead of developing a better public health system with enhanced health budget, 12th five-year plan document has unveiled plans to hand over health care system to private institutions. The 12th plan document causes concern over Rashtriya Swasthya Bhima Yojana being used as a medium to hand over public funds to the private sector through an insurance route, some experts feel. There is also a growing feeling among the people that this has also incentivized unnecessary treatment leading to increased costs and premia. Already, there are complaints about high transaction cost for this scheme due to insurance intermediaries. It appears that RSBY does not take into consideration state specific variation in disease profiles and health needs. Though acknowledged in the report, no alternative remedy has been suggested.

Also, there is no reference to nutrition as a key component of health and for universal Public Distribution System (PDS) in the plan document or HLEG recommendation. In the section of National Rural Health Mission (NRHM) in the document, the commitment to provide 30-to 50-bed Community Health Centres (CHC) per lakh population is missing from the main text.

It was easy for the government to recruit poor women as ASHA (Accredited Social Health Activist) workers but it has failed to bring doctors, nurses and specialist in this area. ASHA workers, coming mainly from a poor economic strata of society, are given incentives based on performance. Even the 12th plan doesn't give any solace.

To sum up, it is revealed that successive administrative and political reforms have conveniently bypassed training citizens and local bodies to actively participate in healthcare. It's a situation where people are not enabled to identify poor quality, speak up and debate. An urgent need has therefore arisen for the health system to fill that role on behalf of the people. This, some aver, can be achieved by decentralization of healthcare governance.

India's health scenario is characterized by a very small Government expenditure on this sector amounting to only 1.2% of GDP. Maternal and infant mortality are still very high and hardly 70% of child births are attended to by skilled health workers. Although India's life expectancy of its population has risen in the last seven decades, it is still no match to countries like China, Thailand and Sri Lanka. Child malnutrition, poor sanitation and rapidly rising burden of non-communicable diseases are other challenges being faced by the Indian Health Sector.

Half the country still does not have proper access to sanitation and potable drinking water facilities. There is high indoor air pollution which again affects women and children mainly. There is high incidence of drug resistant tuberculosis, malaria, dengue, chikungunya etc. **It is also startling that the country's richest families are also having child mal-nutrition which means it is not a question of affordability, rather it is a question of lack of awareness as well.** We are talking every now and then of demographic dividend but if 65-70 million children are having stunted growth, they will not be a dividend but a national curse, because they become prone to diabetes, and heart attacks.

Furthermore, our health care system is becoming unaffordable very fast. 70% of the people spend out of their own pockets. High costs are characterized both by the outpatient fees as well as medicines and these are not covered by most health insurance policies.

It is not that Indian Government has not responded to the need for health and reforms. Government of India came out with a national health mission in the 12th five year plan and principle of universal world coverage which they tried to test in some pilot districts. They have, even proposed amendments to the national health policy and are trying to bring up some cancer centers, and provide more essential drugs free of cost in public facilities and are trying to expand their insurance programs at the state level but this may not be sufficient.

India cannot provide quality health care to all its citizens in an affordable manner unless more and more private sector is brought in to supplement governmental effort as a service provider. The goals need to be specific as the country has to ensure payment linked deliveries from the service providers for efficient, as well as effective provision of services. It is a global trend that Government pays for the poor in a much focused manner and multiple sources of financials are pooled into a single risk pool. Furthermore the government aims at providing low cost drugs/vaccines and affordable technologies in health sector directly or through private sector.

It is not that in India there has been no attempt by the Private sector to provide low cost and high quality health care, there are many examples like Arvind Eye Care, L.V. Prasad Eye Institute, Life Spring Hospitals, Vatsalyam etc. But these remain as the few islands in a large desert of inadequate and poor health services.

Another alternative is to develop and propagate Indian system of Medicine, officially recognized system namely, Ayurveda, Yoga, Naturopathy, Suddha, Unnani and Homoeopathy (Ayush). This system of Health care has a number of comparative strengths including a holistic approach, personalized system of care, fewer side effects and affordability.

In fact a separate department had been created for this purpose way back in 1995 for encouraging the scientific research and education, laying down pharmacopoeial standards to ensure quality drugs evolving good laboratories and manufacturing practice regulating education standards etc.

In spite of all the efforts put in by Government to popularise and strengthen the AYUSH as an alternative system for providing affordable Health Care system, it somehow seems to be not have taken off at desired level except in few States like Kerala, Tamil Nadu and West Bengal. The corrective measures are required to be taken to make this system successful and popular whether it is by creating country wide network of hospitals and dispensaries or to ensure standardization of education and curriculum or the quality control and quality assurance issues with reference to ASU drugs.

It is heartening to note that the holistic benefits of Yoga and meditation are being propagated at international as well as national level by observing 21st June as International Yoga Day on the initiative taken by the Prime Minister.

The Government of India needs to ask a basic question to it that since its finances are restricted, where it should put its money. Should it be on preventive health care or on primary health care or in creating hospitals? It needs to prioritize.

As the age old adage goes that 'prevention is better than cure'. It holds very good in the context of preventive health care measures including nutrition, universal immunization and sanitation. The Modi Government has launched very ambitious programmes for cleanliness namely, 'Swachch Bharat Mission' and Mission Indradhanush for universal immunization. Mission Indradhanush aims to immunize all children against seven vaccination preventable diseases by 2020. Learning from the successful implementation of the polio programme, the process of immunization has been taken up in a mission mode to accelerate the immunization by 5% or more children every year.

Swachch Bharat Mission is a national campaign launched by the Government aiming at accomplishing the vision of a clean India by Oct, 2019; 150th birth anniversary of Mahatma Gandhi. Its specific objectives are, elimination of open defication conversion of unsanitary toilets to pour flush toilets, eradication of manual scavenging, 100% collection and disposal of municipal solid waste, behavioral change in people regarding healthy sanitation practices and generation of awareness about sanitation and its linkage to public health.

The Prime Minister exhorted the people to make this campaign a mass movement. The programme aims to construct

12 crore toilets in rural India by 2019. It is heartening to note that 14 Private Companies and 71 PSUs have come forward to support the construction of as many as 3,195 and 86,781 toilets respectively.

As far as the problem of child mal/under nutrition is concerned, it is a serious matter, but one that can be tackled easily by awareness generation through a mission mode approach all over the country including both rich and poor. Under nutrition is not about food only. It is about sanitation, suboptimal feeding, non-nutritious feeding and ignoring the concept of energy providing diets. It should be an eye opener for us that in India diarrhea is the biggest killer of children. We can also not ignore the fact that the human brain develops fully within the first two years and unless children are fed well, there can be no national health in the real sense of the term.

This was just a glimpse of the challenges in the Health Sector. Now lets have a book at another core sector – the Education in India.

◻

EDUCATION IN INDIA

In India, education is provided by the public sector as well as the private sector, with control and funding coming from three levels: central, state, and local. Under the constitution free and compulsory education is provided as a fundamental right to children between the ages of 6 and 14.

India has certainly progressed in increasing primary education attendance rate and expanding literacy to approximately three-quarters of the population in the 7-10 age group, by 2011. India's improved education system is claimed to be one of the main contributors to its economic development. Much of the progress, especially in higher education and scientific research, has been credited to various public institutions.

At the primary and secondary level, India has a large private school system complementing government run schools, with 29% of students receiving private education in the 6 to 14 age group. Certain post-secondary technical schools are also private. The private education market in India had a revenue of US$ 450 million in 2008, but is projected to be a US$ 40 billion market.

As per the Annual Status of Education Report (ASER) 2012, 96.5% of all rural children between the ages of 6-14 were enrolled in school. This is the fourth annual survey to report enrolment above 96%. Another report from 2013 stated that there were 229 million students enrolled in different accredited urban and rural schools of India, from Class I to XII, representing an increase of 2.3 million students over 2002 total enrolment, and a 19% increase in girl's enrolment. While quantitatively India is inching closer to universal education, the quality of its education has been questioned particularly in its government run school system. Some of the reasons for the poor quality include absence of around 25 percent of teachers every day. States of India have introduced tests and education assessment system to identify and improve such schools.

While there are private schools in India, it is important to note that they are highly regulated in terms of what they can teach, in what form they can operate (must be a non-profit to run any accredited educational institution). So, the difference in government schools and private schools can actually be misguiding.

In India's education system, a significant number of seats are reserved under affirmative action policies for the historically disadvantaged Scheduled Castes and Scheduled Tribes and Other Backward Classes. In universities, colleges, and similar institutions affiliated to the federal government, there is a minimum 50% of reservations applicable to these disadvantaged groups, at the state level it can vary. Maharashtra had 73% reservation in 2014, the highest in reservations in India.

India's higher education system is the third largest in the world, after China and the United States. The main governing body at the tertiary level is the University Grants Commission (India), which enforces its standards, advises the government, and helps coordinate between the centre and the state.

Accreditation for higher learning is overseen by 12 autonomous institutions established by the University Grants Commission. In India, education system is reformed. In the future, India will be one of the largest education hubs of the world.

As per some estimates, in 2012, India had 152 central universities, 316 state universities, and 191 private universities. Other institutions include 33,623 colleges, including 1,800 exclusive women's colleges, functioning under these universities and institutions, and 12748 Institutions offering Diploma Courses. The emphasis in the tertiary level of education lies on science and technology.

Indian educational institutions by 2004 consisted of a large number of technology institutes. Distance learning is also a feature of the Indian higher education system. The Government has launched Rashtriya Uchchattar Shiksha Abhiyan to provide strategic funding to State higher and technical institutions. A total of 316 state public universities and 13,024 colleges will be covered under it.

Some institutions of India, such as the Indian Institutes of Technology (IITs), Indian Institute of Science and University of Mumbai have been globally acclaimed for their standard of undergraduate education in engineering. The IITs enroll about 10,000 students annually and the alumni have contributed to both the growth of the private sector and the public sectors of India. However, the IIT's have not had significant impact on fundamental scientific research and innovation. Several other institutes of fundamental research such as the Indian Association for the Cultivation of Science (IACS), Indian Institute of Science (IISc), Tata Institute of Fundamental Research (TIFR), Harishchandra Research Institute (HRI), are acclaimed for their standard of research in basic sciences and mathematics.

However, India has failed to produce world class universities both in the private sector or the public sector. Besides top rated universities which provide highly competitive world class education to their pupils, India is also home to many universities which have been founded with the sole objective of making easy money. Regulatory authorities like UGC and AICTE have been trying very hard to extirpate the menace of private universities which are running courses without any affiliation or recognition. Indian Government has failed to check on these education shops, which are run by big businessmen and politicians. Many private colleges and universities do not fulfil the required criterion by the Government and central bodies (UGC, AICTE, MCI, BCI etc.) and take students for a ride. For example, many institutions in India continue to run unaccredited courses as there is no legislation strong enough to ensure legal action against them.

Quality assurance mechanisms have failed to stop misrepresentations and malpractices in higher education. At the same time regulatory bodies have been accused of corruption, specifically in the case of deemed-universities. In this context of lack of solid quality assurance mechanism, institutions need to step-up and set higher standards of self-regulation.

Higher Education in India is a must for India to become the global economic power. The challenges of higher education mainly are in the form of an inflexible curriculum structures, examination-centric evaluation system and outdated techniques of teaching leading to disinterest and boredom in students. There is huge gap in research infrastructure with more focus on creating buildings than other important requirements. The academicians have become ossified in their thinking and approach. Regulatory bodies have left very little autonomy to educational institutions. What country needs is, various kinds of institutions, some of them focusing on careers and others on research areas. There should be a balance of quality and quantity and continuous innovation should be order of the day. The private sector needs to be involved in a big way but mindless profiteering amounting to loot needs to scrupulously avoid. **Let those developing educational institutions treat this as a noble venture and not as yet another commercial enterprise geared to abominal profiteering. A long term vision is the need of the hour for creating global level universities with universal presence and international enrolment.**

Creating global presence and international enrolment. The funding philosophy patterns have to be changed. There needs to be more collaboration of Institutions within India and at global level which can lead to the creation of a National hub of knowledge. This will also encourage strong linkages with industry and create a more vibrant higher education system.

India needs to create a more rich learning experience by creating apprenticeships in all under graduate programs so that students get a lateral entry into lucrative professions. There is an inherent need for creating a relationship between entrepreneurs and industry for which industry can sponsor creation of 'entrepreneurs' development centers' in all institutions of higher learning. It is also matter of deep regret that learning in India by and large ends in Institutions itself whereas it should be a lifelong learning mode. There is need to use technology for giving learning to all in whatever sectors they want. Instead of allowing our students to go abroad for higher studies, India should concentrate on becoming the global hub of higher education. Indian institutions need to enter into collaborative ventures with overseas educational bodies for creating more and more capacities domestically as well as in foreign lands.

Capacity expansion will need capital and technology infusion from private sector in this area. **All regulatory authorities should focus on the outcome rather than regulate inputs and stifle the autonomy of institutions. The functions and roles of regulatory bodies need to be changed and they ought to be trained for the changed roles.** The institutions of higher learning should be made more accountable and be asked to induct global practices of excellence and establish global bench marks of learning. The Nation should try to attract the best minds to doing research in Indian institutions of higher learning.

Education needs to be linked to employment. The focus should be on learning for earning and the emphasis of skill training should be to creating more and more skill development universities and careers/placement centers. Unless this is done, any rise in employment opportunities is going to remain a pipe dream. This aspect has been understood by the planners of Indian Higher Education System. The 12th Five Year Plan document has laid a special emphasis on expansion of skill based programmes in higher education. The scheme of community colleges was launched in 2013-14 in a pilot mode.

Realising skills and knowledge as the driving forces of economic growth and the urgent necessity for developing skills and creating work ready manpower on large scale, the Government decided to set up a skill development ministry and launched new Kaushal Kendra Scheme investing massive funds for Skill India Programme for enabling the youth to work efficiently and become self employed entrepreneurs.

Fortunately, the Prime Minister is well aware of the necessity of providing good quality jobs to India's youth and is wanting to increase the educational quality and opportunity for 600 million young Indians. **It is also true that there is no universal model of development in higher education.** It is just the effectiveness of the system which is required. Asia has done a lot of catching up with the west except that India is still far behind even among of the leading nations in Asia.

The problem of generating employment is very serious. Even at present employment demand is slowing down across the country both in organized and unorganized sectors. It is also due to slow down in economy but another reason is that Indian businessmen prefer less labor intensive activities because of the multiplicity and cumbersomeness of labor laws. The problem will become more serious if one looks at the next five decades because population and consequently working hands will increase.

So if the necessary employment opportunities cannot be generated, it will lead to chaos. How Government decides to tackle this issue needs to be seen but there can be a few suggestions. The creation of road infrastructure, telecom infrastructure, tourism, labour intensive manufacturing, mining, construction and real estate – all these areas if revitalized can lead to generation of additional employment which is badly required. We need to provide employment to at least 500 lakh people in next five years by the Government and the private sector. This may require reforms of labor laws and labour market, but that is inevitable.

❑

TOURISM – THE GREAT MULTIPLIER

The Government has already started taking the right baby steps for getting the country back on track. It is seized with the urgent need for policy requirements or changes. Ease of doing business India has become one of the top priorities for the administration. However, we go by the World Banks' index of business environment, India currently has a very low ranking, which means India is still saddled with a very difficult or cumbersome business environment. The factors which need to change are; to have rational tax demands, remove all uncertainty regarding rules governing investments, reducing time lag and speeding up the clearance processes, ensuring protection against extortion by the Mafia – all this needs to be done before anything else. The government has already started removing rigidities in labour laws and labour ranks but a lot more needs to be done. Infrastructure of all sorts has to be put in place. There is need to provide least cost coverage by bank credit.

India's manufacturing sector policy needs to be overhauled which can only be done by providing two principle factors of production i.e. labour and land at affordable rates. At present the cost of labour and land, both are high which does not facilitate mass manufacturing, but there is need also for the industries to make things better at their level. They need to adopt the industrial training institutes who tackle the skill shortages. They also need to sponsor training institutes as well as the research for industry. A large scale internship programme also depends upon the industry and not the Government. Industry also needs to self-regulate and be aware of cross capitalism. They need to nurture their works as well as suppliers. They also need to attain global level of competitiveness and stop asking for undue protectionism from the Government. While all this is being done, should not we be looking at another sector, a great multiplier of incomes and employment for which are have abundant opportunity and resources. That's 'tourism'.

Tourism contributes to the economy of a Nation by generating income, employment and foreign exchange. It has been recognized as a significant factor in the economy of developed as well as developing countries. Tourism affects both the host country as well as the destination country from where the tourists are coming. The tourist is an ideal instrument for exporting social and cultural models leading to a global integration. The life style of a tourist has a chain effect on the host community. Among the export earnings of India, Tourism is the third largest earner. Let us look at the figures of foreign tourist arrivals and foreign exchange earnings from tourism for India in this chapter.

The foreign tourist arrivals in India during the year 2008 were 5.37 million as compared to 5.08 million in 2007 registering a growth of 5.6 per cent. During the period January to March 2009, the growth rate was minus 13.8 per cent as compared to the corresponding period of 2008, this is the effect of recent global meltdown and economic down turn. The foreign exchange earnings from tourism during 2008 in US dollar terms are estimated at 11.75 billion as compared to 10.73 during 2007, registering a growth of 5.6 PER CENT. During the period January to March 2009, the growth rate was minus 13.8 per cent as compared to the corresponding period of 2008, this is the effect of recent global melt down and economic down turn. The foreign exchange earnings from tourism during 2008 in US dollar terms are estimated at 11.75 billion as compared to 10.73 during 2007, registering a growth of 9.5 per cent. During the period January to March, 2009, understandably the growth rate is – 30 per cent because of the global melt down and consequent lesser arrivals of the foreign tourists.

But it is not only the foreign tourist who constitutes the main revenue stream of tourism earnings in India, even domestic tourism has grown substantially during the last few years due to increase in income levels and emergence of a dynamic urban middle class. However even the Ministry of Tourism, Government of India does not have precise estimates of total domestic tourists traffic in the country, but as per the figures reported by the States/Union Territory Governments to Government of India, the domestic tourists during 2007 are estimated to be 527 million showing a growth of 14 per cent as compared to 2006 (Annual Report).

The World Trade Organisation (WTO) has named India along with China as one of the fastest growing tourism industries for the next 15 years. India ranks among top five destinations from 167 countries. India is projected as having potential of dollar 24 billion annual foreign exchange earnings through tourism by 2015. While we agree with the potential of tourism to provide income and employment to our people but without sustainability aspect being taken care of tourism or even the whole concept of growth or development will be useless so let's have a look at what is sustainability and how does it apply to tourism or even national development so that our future generations do not have to pay for our greed or follies.

Sustainable tourism is a term in which the concept of sustainability evolves from sustainable development. There are some authors who, while explaining the concept of sustainability, have said that sustainable development is a potential slogan rather than an analytical tool. It may be viewed as a philosophy, a plan or strategy or a product. This is not to denigrate its utility in fostering dialogue among groups and individuals whose interests may at the first sight appear to be incompatible. Thus it may be a catalyst for discussion, compromise and the identification of appropriate trade-offs between competing interests in the development scenario.

Development refers to broad perspectives concerning appropriate future states and the means of achieving them. As a process it emphasizes the methods which might be employed to expand or bring out the potentials or capabilities of a phenomenon. A development plan sets out specific steps through which desirable future states are to be achieved. And development, as a product indicates the level of achievement of an individual or society, as in the developed, developing and underdeveloped countries.

Development as a term has changed over time. The term development is value-laden, incorporating a mix of material and moral ideas encompassing both present and future states – what currently exists, as well as what might be brought into being in the future. In its early formulations it focused primarily upon economic matters. However, definitions have broadened over time and development has gradually come to be viewed as a social as well as an economic process which involves the progressive improvement of conditions, and the fulfillment of a potential. Now, in addition to economic issues, it encompasses social, environmental and ethical considerations, and its measurement may incorporate indicators like poverty, unemployment, inequality and self-reliance. Notions of development have encompassed economic growth viz. structural change, autonomous industrialization and self-reliance, and have been pitched at a variety of scales from the individual to the regional, national and even international.

However, growth and development are not to be regarded as the same thing, since economic growth as measured by gross national product per capita can occur with an increase in poverty, unemployment and inequality, whereas development cannot exist without some betterment. In its most basic form development is concerned with human betterment through improvement in life styles and life time opportunities. However, it is contentious as to how this is to be done and so the term has come to have strong political underpinnings.

As is the case with sustainable development, the notion of development has also come to be used in rather different ways as a philosophy, as a process, as a plan and as a product.

Sustainable development can be viewed as a component of the alternative development paradigm discussed above. As in development as a whole, it may be regarded as a philosophy, a plan or a strategy, or a product. It has been defined by the Brundtland Commission as "development that meets the needs of the present without compromising the ability of future generations to meet their own needs." Sustainable development had received widespread support because it appeared that it was an idea whose time had come reflecting a convergence of scientific knowledge, economics and sociopolitical activity and environmental realities that would guide human development into the twenty-first century. This may be because it was a concept which acknowledged the needs of the world's poor and the limitations imposed on development by current levels of technical ability, social organization and environmental variability. It has received strong bureaucratic support at all levels, from local grassroots organizations to international agencies, partly because it reinforces a world view of economic growth as the engine of both development and environmental protection. Again, it lends legitimacy to the free-market economy, belief in trickle-down economics and the benefits of technological progress. It refers to opportunities for a wide ranging action at all levels.

New institutions, policies and programs which may be initiated under the guise of sustainable development provide significant opportunities to expand power bases acquire additional resources and enhance prestige on the part of bureaucrats and administrators. At the same time, sustainable development has been criticized on ideological grounds as promoting maintenance of the western capitalist system, as being ambiguous and as a concept that tries to do something for everyone by tinkering at the margin of the economic system which originally created the problems that the concept is supposed to help address. At the extreme, **one might regard sustainable development as an oxymoron: sustainable, implying a state which can be maintained is ongoing, perhaps even unchanging; while development implying change.**

Maintaining change, ongoing change or unchanging changes are not clear messages! On the other hand, the ambiguity of the term potentially permits flexibility and fine-tuning to meet the needs of different places and cultures. It encourages greater consideration of the environment, and more effectively integrates environmental and economic matters in decision-making by encouraging dialogue' between individuals with different perspectives. The concept is also in line with the community and participatory emphasis of much tourism literature.

But unfortunately the emphasis of many 'Third World' governments is not predominantly on the poor but on large-scale projects, both in tourism and other economic sectors, and generally provides little opportunity for local inputs. Thus the imprecision of the term has also been conducive to the formation of a gap between rhetoric and action or reality, between policy and implementation.

Imprecision has also helped disguise the fundamental re-orientation which is required if sustainable development is to be sought and achieved. The scientific and technical approach which has resulted in great advances in knowledge has been achieved through adoption of a narrow focus and reductionism. In contrast, sustainable development advocates a holistic approach and an appreciation of the inter-connectedness of phenomena of nature and life.

Furthermore, humans have often been viewed as being separate from nature, which is there for humans to exploit, manage and control. **Sustainable development implies that ultimately, humans and environment are an indivisible part of each other.** A concept which was propounded so simply and beautifully by Pandit Deen Dayal Upadhayaya in his Philosophy of 'Ekatam Manav-wad'.

Conventional economics encourage people to act against their own best interests by placing greater value on present rather than on future consumption. Growth in production and consumption is often equated with progress, while economic growth is still regarded as the best if not the only way to meet society's needs. Thus a belief in the value of modernity, the power of science and technology, and the law of supply and demand has been promulgated by western society and exported to other parts of the world. Such ideas do not fit snugly with the notions of sustainable development at all.

Will the recent global meltdown and economic downturn and the socio-economic fluctuation that it has brought in its wake have an impact on tourism, especially the sustainability factor? If so, will it be positive or negative? To find answers to these questions, it would be worthwhile to retrace one's steps and briefly evaluate some past experiences before taking current realities into account. On the negative side, tourist flows worldwide experienced a severe decline in the early 1990s as discretionary incomes fell and unemployment rose.

Economic recovery was slow and patchy, matched by a positive, response in tourist activity, and regional contrasts in a return to previous levels. But on the positive side, the shock of economic recession and subsequent restructuring of national economies helped focus renewed attention on the longer-term potential of tourism for boosting economic activity and employment. Butler remarked that reductions in public sector expenditure which accompanied widespread economic restructuring prompted governments to capture the attention of tourism industry representatives and encourage private sector investment in tourism projects, either separately or as joint ventures. Construction and operation of casinos in several Australian states are examples. It is too early to assess the total impact of the current recession but it would be safe to assume, in the light of earlier experiences that negative factors will be much bigger and better organized than ever before, with technological innovations and immense information networking at its command.

Moreover, the perception of society as a whole has undergone favorable changes in relation to tourism. Talking about the relationship between societal changes and cyclical things like economic changes, it is well known that societal changes normally do not exhibit the same cyclical characteristics as those of an economic nature. Rather, they are evolutionary and cumulative, and sometimes almost imperceptible. Ageing of western populations has been accompanied by a measure of affluence, increased unobligated time, and the desire to remain active among older age groups. It is no longer unusual to find 'elderly' people undertaking strenuous (and expensive) tours, uninhibited by the misperceptions, restrictions and taboos of a past time. At the other end of the demographic spectrum it is becoming common place for younger, unaccompanied people to enter the tourist flows.

Youth tourism, stimulated by a range of motives and underpinned again by 'free' time, energy, spirit of adventure, and perhaps restrained expectations, is a growing segment of the tourism market. Changes in attitudes to marriage and family, to gender, sex and racial discrimination, are additional forces helping to fashion the tourism of the 1990s. Whereas socio-economic fluctuations can create difficulties for the tourism sector, those same societal changes and economic adjustments can lead to a more discerning tourism clientele.

A greater role for communities in tourism developments and more searching scrutiny of tourism proposals should help achieve the objective of sustainability.

Sustainable development is certainly distinct from sustainable tourism. Widespread interest in sustainable development has captured the attention of tourism industry representatives and researchers and has resulted in the promulgation of sustainable tourism. Butler, who is one of the most articulate critics of sustainable tourism, has defined it as follows: "Tourism which is in a form can maintain its viability in an area for an indefinite period or time". He contrasts this with a definition of sustainable development in the context of tourism as "tourism which is developed and maintained in an area (community, environment) in such a manner and on such a scale that it remains viable over an indefinite period and does not degrade or alter the environment (human and physical) in which it exists to such a degree that it prohibits the successful development and well-being [sic] of other activities and processes".

The distinction is critical and not grasped by many advocates of sustainable tourism. It is essentially the distinction between a single-sector and a multiple-sector approach to development. The first definition places the emphasis on all the perpetuation of tourism neglecting other potential uses of scarce resources. However, tourism competes with other activities for the use of limited resources of land, water, labour and capital.

The appropriation of resources may be in the narrow interests of the tourism industry, but may not be in the best interests of the broader community of interests of which tourism is only a part. In fact diversity, whether it be in economy or biology, is likely to promote rather than detract from sustainability more broadly conceived. The second definition acknowledges that tourism is unlikely to be the sole user of resources and that a balance must be found between tourism and other existing and potential. How can one then recognize an enduring option ahead of the activities in the interests of sustainable development?

In other words, trade-offs between sectors may be necessary in the interests of the greater good of the country. But the moot question is: What is this greater good and what is to be sustained and who is to decide this? These are intractable questions. Should one be trying to sustain individuals, communities, regions or nations; experiences for tourists, incomes for business or life-style for residents; individual enterprises, economic sectors or whole economies and production systems; economic activities, cultural expressions or environmental conditions? Should all existing tourism developments be sustained or is it preferable that some be allowed to decline gracefully to be replaced by other activities? And should these new activities be tourism based so that one could speak of sustainable tourism even though the form of tourism has changed and the new form might not contribute to the broader goal of sustainable development?

If the goal for sustainable development is to meet human needs, then an elaboration of these needs is required. Which specific needs are of concern? At what point are needs satisfactorily met? In case of conflicting but valid needs, what are the needs that should take priority and what is the criteria to determine this? Is tourism to be regarded as a need of the present generation or is it an instrument which is to be employed to achieve sustainable development for other people at a future time?

The long-term perspective of sustainable tourism is encouraged by the sustainable development-doctrine and is both the strength and weakness of the concept. The strength is that it would support the precautionary and tie-in principles. The former advocates keeping opportunities open and not foreclosing options in the interests of short-term gains. The latter encourages taking actions, such as water conservation and the requirement that structures should be away from coasts, which does not make sense now but which increases resilience to future environmental perturbations. On the other hand, in the absence of a crystal ball, it is virtually impossible to determine which experiences will be desired by future tourists or residents, or to assess the influences of technological change for sustainability. How might one recognize a sustainable option in advance of the achievement of the associated sustainable tomorrow given growing populations, emerging technologies and changing tastes?

While most would agree that if tourism is to contribute to sustainable development it must be economically viable, environmentally sensitive and culturally appropriate, the forms which this might take are likely to vary with location. This in turn means that it will be difficult to come up with useful principles for tourism development in the context of socio-cultural choices which are true for all places and all times.

"In the long run we are all ultimately dead" may once have been an acceptable axiom for some industrialists and economists, but it can no longer be considered an appropriate policy maxim. Over the last two decades, policy-makers, planners, industrialists and economists have become increasingly aware of the imperative need to consider bottle environmental implications of proposed developments' and also aspirations (indeed the rights) of future generations to have the opportunities to make their own use of scarce resources.

Having an international perspective on tourism one has to see how it has evolved over a period of time. Since the beginning of the 1980s there has been a growing number of international reports, statements and accords concerning the present and future well-being of Planet Earth. Some of these meetings have focused specifically on the role of tourism as an agent of development in the context of its wider environmental implications. Notable among these international initiatives are the 1980 World Conservation Strategy, which stressed the need for sustainability in the use of natural resources; the Brandt Commission in the same year emphasized the need for development to include 'care for the environment'; the Manila Declaration which inter alia pointed out that natural resources are of common heritage, and stressed the need for tourism-development to be environmentally sound; and the Brundtland Report 1987, which indicated a path towards sustainable development with economic growth.

International concern for the environmental effects of development in its various modes and also for the effects of development on the socio-cultural choices and about the life of the affected communities has stimulated a plethora of papers by academics and practitioners alike. Indeed it could be argued that in many cases these papers have helped in creating public awareness and concern.

Unfortunately, not all of the recent literary outpourings have been helpful in clarifying the issues. **In particular, the introduction of some new terminologies and definitions has helped to cloud understanding and make agreements more difficult to reach. Among these misleading terminologies should be included the ambiguous phrase 'alternative tourism'.**

At the Zakopane meeting, participants readily recognized that the concept of 'alternative tourism' had achieved some credence in describing it as a more benign alternative to mass or conventional tourism, but they pointed out the imprecise character of the term **Alternative Tourism**. Instead, the participants recommended that phrases such as 'alternative forms of tourism' or 'tourism alternatives' should be used to refer to the multiplicity of different forms of the same. One valuable outcome of the Zakopane Conference was the publication of Tourism Alternatives (Smith and Eadington, 1992), a selection of readings, some of which are already important state-of-the-art papers and others which may, well become seminal works in the field. The participants at the Tamransett Conference reached a similar conclusion in rejecting the term 'alternative tourism' and instead the phrase 'responsible tourism' was recommended to be adopted.

The concept of sustainability is inherent in many papers on alternative tourism, eco-tourism, green tourism, soft tourism, nature tourism, etc., but the term itself gained more common usage and acceptance with the publication of the Brundtland Report, our Common Future. The Brundtland Commission defined 'sustainable development' as a process of change in which there is exploitation of resources, and the direction of investments. The orientation of technological development, and institutional changes are made consistent 'with future as well as present needs', and as 'meeting the needs of the present without compromising the ability of future generations to meet their own needs'.

Whereas the concepts of the Brundtland Report are probably acceptable to all but the most purblind and self interested developers and politicians, major problems arise in defining methods of implementation and in reconciling all of the interests involved. In this context, an interesting Action Strategy for Sustainable Development' was prepared by the Tourism stream Action Strategy Commission of the Globe '90 in its Conference, on sustainable development held in April 1990 in Vancouver, Canada. A reproduction of the draft is provided in Ins keep. Also, in Canada, D'Amore gives an interesting account of the progress made in that country towards achieving guidelines, codes of ethics and practical means of responding to the Brundtland Report. De Kadt (1992) recognizes that whereas there is a need for future growth in some countries and regions in order to improve the material well-being of the resident population, 'policy-makers can... promote sustainability by constantly striving to make the conventional more sustainable' and that many 'alternative forms of tourism' will continue to evolve but, for economic reasons, will 'almost inevitably....(ride)...piggyback on the more cost-effective forms of the conventional, integrated international tourism industry'. His final sentence 'how to coax that behemoth into less destructive behavior is surely the main task ahead' could well form the theme of any major conference. **Since the Zakopane and Tamransett Conferences, academics have continued to publish books and the new Journals of Alternative Tourism have been launched.** In addition, a spasmodic but very valuable correspondence on sustainability in tourism is being conducted by trinetters on e-mail. This correspondence reflects the thoughts and ideas of the participants in an un-published form. It is very much to be hoped that the trinetters will eventually use their correspondence to form the basis of a publication which will be a useful contribution to the concept and spread of sustainability.

The major problem with the concept of sustainability is how to measure the social cost-benefit analysis involved in the concept. So far economists have contributed relatively little to the debate on sustainable tourism and have emerged with little kudos for their part in the development of tourism. It is easy to cast them together with developers as the villains of the act in that they have provided theoretical, conceptual and mathematical justifications for past growth and development without considering the environmental and socio-cultural consequences of their recommendations.

There may be an element of truth in this viewpoint. **Economists are concerned with the allocation of scarce resources which have alternative uses, but it should be remembered that economists per se do not lay down the policy prescriptions for the use of these resources. Policy guidelines and objectives are laid down by the relevant governmental or international bodies and these stated aims govern economists' recommendations regarding the allocation of resources.** If, for example, a government wishes to maximize the income levels or employment opportunities for its resident population, an economist's task is to recommend optimum allocation or redistribution of resources to achieve those objectives. Also it should be remembered that herein lies one of the major difficulties faced by economists: the cost-benefit analysis. Economic models and techniques exist to evaluate most impact situations, but economists working in isolation are not in a position to express many of the factors involved in money terms. Perhaps the best known and one of the least understood, an economic model is social cost benefit analysis. This term is often confused by non-economists with financial analysis which, in the context of development, describes a detailed study of the revenue and costs which accrue to a developer if a new project or set of projects is to be undertaken.

Financial analysis places the emphasis on the financial revenue and costs accruing to the developers and not to the affected community or to the country as a whole. All other benefits and costs are external to the analysis and accrue elsewhere. On the other hand social cost-benefit analysis takes a wider and deeper view of the benefits and costs, being concerned with the community as a whole, including future generations. It is not concerned with the profitability of the development to the company or consortium, but with the net benefit to the host community.

The theoretical and conceptual basis of social cost-benefit analysis and the methodologies for assessing and measuring data have been the subject of much debate and investigation by economists throughout the second half of this century. The literature is extensive, but a flavour of the concept and its usefulness and limitations can be gleaned from Prest and Turvey, Layerd, Little and Mirrlees. The technique has been used widely and can investigate simultaneously a large number of alternative uses of the same resources in continuance of the status quo. Indeed the greater the number of alternative uses that are investigated, the more meaningful and helpful are the results. The principle weakness of the approach, as previously mentioned, is the inability of economists to recognize, assess and measure factors such as ecological and socio-cultural implications which do not have readily apparent monetary values.

In essence, social cost-benefit analysis involves assessing and measuring (in a common monetary unit) the consequences of the proposed forms of development. All of the identified and measured benefits and costs are discounted back to their present value to provide a common yardstick of measurement. For islands and small States, one of the measures recommended is the foreign exchange equivalent and value of the money in the hands of the government. The discount rate-used in social cost-benefit analysis is quite different from that used by private sector developers. Whereas the latter uses a discount rate which reflects both the rate of borrowing money and the risk factors involved, social cost-benefit analysts use a rate which is intended to reflect society's valuation of net benefits in the present time rather than in future.

Indeed, the identification and measurement of externalities are for economists the most difficult aspect of social cost-benefit analysis. Pollution of beaches is a common occurrence in tourism development and economists can assign a monetary value to such occurrences and to the costs of taking preventive or remedial actions. Indeed it is possible to; internalize' this type of cost to the developers themselves by legally enforcing them to take measures to prevent the occurrence of such situations. Nevertheless, many externalities, the theoretical and conceptual basis of social cost-benefit notably ecological effects, are much harder for economists and others analysis and the methodologies for assessing and measuring data to identify or evaluate. Unless such effects can be anticipated and have been the subject of much debate and investigation by the costs of preventative action evaluated, it is impossible to include economists throughout the second half of this century.

It may be, for example, that a proposed development involves the destruction of a specific habitat and in consequence the possible eradication of a particular species of fauna or flora, If, in such cases, some ecologists place an infinite monetary value on the preservation of this threatened species, then it could be argued that the environmental costs of the proposed development would be greater than the net economic benefits, however great these may, be. On the basis of this premise, such development should not be allowed to proceed. In such a situation, however, an economist would not accept the premise that preserving the habitat had an infinite value. Instead, he would wish to calculate and include in the analysis the total costs of recreating the threatened habitat in another suitable location and of preserving the threatened species. Similarly, an investigation of proposed mining developments in a National Park in the UK considered the net benefits accruing to the region over a long time span. During the period of active mining, considerable environmental and other costs would be incurred, especially the impact on the aesthetic appearance of the area. If, however, at the end of the active mining period, the area were to be completely restored at the expense of the developer, then after a few years, there is a powerful influence on modern tourism. Technological breakthrough would be few if any traces of the development. In this case the magnitude of the net present value of the benefits depended partly upon the value attached by the affected population to the environmental damage incurred over the period of mining operations rather than over an indefinitely prolonged period of time.

One of the major benefits of sustainable tourism is that one can minimise the occurrence of damage in it. Long lasting environmental damage is a different consideration. Advances in technology have made it possible for most forms of pollution and many other violations of the environment to be avoided, ameliorated or rectified at a subsequent date. As previously mentioned, such damages can be minimised by imposing legal restrictions and/or financial penalties to the cost to the developer. Admittedly, in some cases, long-term damage may occur and it is essential that a monetary valuation of such damage should be included as a cost in the cost-benefit analysis.

Similarly, social scientists in other disciplines must be prepared to identify and place a valuation on any expected changes in socio-cultural patterns which might result from a proposed development. A minimum social scientist should endeavor to produce a ranking order of such changes. And also there appears to be little merit in undertaking still more ex-post studies, which describe outcomes as being 'good' or 'bad'. **What is needed is the degree of acceptability of any anticipated changes and their perceived costs and benefits to the residents and to the government in order to assist economists in assessing the social benefits and costs involved.**

Again, the most adverse aspects of expected changes can be, offset by forethought and planning, the costs involved can be 'internalized' within the costs of development.

In Mauritius, for example, in order to prevent the disruption by tourists of Sega Dances organized by local communities, they arrange visits by Sega Dance troupes to the major hotels. Examples of such provisions for visitors exist in other tourist destinations too, for example, among the Indians of North America.

Technology also has a great impact on sustainability and a powerful influence on modern tourism. Technological breakthrough can change the sustainability status of a tourism business or destination overnight, but they can also offer effective means towards long-term sustainability in an ecological sense. **Tourism, as with many other sectors of the economy, has experienced the shock of technological change. Improvements in transport and communications have decreased the friction of distance and made the greater part of the globe accessible.** The advent of long-distance, large capacity aircraft, has made mass tourism a reality at the international scale, and with it the capacity to make or break intermediate points in all air routes. Airlines crossing the Pacific now routinely over fly Nadi Airport in Fiji with detrimental effects on the economy of the Islands. Honolulu is frequently bypassed by long-range aircraft flying directly point-to-point. Even on the North American an inland, an airline's choice of hub can have repercussions for regional economies based in part on servicing aircraft, equipment, crews and passengers. High speed, computer-based communication and reservation facilities are now an integral part of the global tourism network. Not only do these facilities enable instantaneous links across the world, but also they have added immeasurably to the levels of awareness, both of tourists and those serving the travelling public.

With awareness and exposure come stimulated demand for hitherto little known destinations. This, coupled with the ability to move vast numbers of people great distances in relatively short periods of time, means that few parts of the planet can any longer be regarded as out of the reach of tourists. This is a somewhat a disturbing prospect, given the shrinking availability of sites to cater for the growing interest and involvement in eco-tourism, nature-based tourism and unspoiled destinations. The natural environment is a growing magnet for tourists, and great care will be needed in managing access to and use of natural sites so that technological advances do not threaten ecological sustainability.

Perhaps the most exciting and powerful tool of technology has yet to impact fully on the tourism scene is by way of the Internet's World Wide Web. The potential of the rapidly expanding Internet to create and disseminate knowledge relevant to tourism marketing is receiving increasing attention. Accessed through the Internet, interactive media can create new sales opportunities for tourism enterprises and services. Hawkins stresses the importance for the tourism industry of understanding how to use the Internet, the on-line services, and interactive electronic media, to market and sell travel products. Already, travel companies have established itinerary planning systems, and tour operators, travel suppliers and destination management groups have pages on the World Wide Web. It was estimated that more than 100 million people would be connected to the Internet by the year 2000, with instant access to relevant, in-depth, up-to-date information about any country or destination. Today perhaps the figure is much larger than anticipated.

Used interactively, the Internet offers the facility to select tourism sites and activities based on complete product information, and the promise of a fulfilling tourism experience, yet in a sustainable environmental context.

One of the significant economic features of tourism is that income earned at places of residence or work is spent in far off places of pleasure or places visited by these tourists. Consequently, tourism is responsible for transfer of huge sums of money from the generating to the receiving destinations. This payment then creates additional funds for being spent on the local economy. Thus tourism represents expenditure or income the same way as large merchandise trade imports or exports. Globally tourism constitutes a major item in world trade that has shown much faster rate of growth in recent years than world trade in goods.

The money spent by tourists tends to percolate through many levels. The expenditure incurred by the tourist stimulates flow of income in the local economy through several streams. It generates additional income at each round of spending and this has a multiplier effect. It has been estimated that the multiplier effect of tourism expenditure is one of the highest and therefore the most sought after. It is therefore not surprising that a number of countries now like to promote tourism as a means of solving their economic problems.

Tourism has tremendous employment potential. The type of employment promoted by tourism varies from that of highly trained managers of deluxe hotels to room boys, transport workers, sales girls, artisans and others. The activity also has a high potential for self-employment in a variety of ancillaries such as horticulture, handicrafts, handlooms, guides etc. **As an activity tourism is highly suited to women particularly if they also have to look after their families and children as is the case in most developing countries.** While tourism also upgrades human skills some of the skills required and promoted by this activity are not difficult to master.

SUGGESTED STRATEGIES FOR SUSTAINABLE COMMUNITY-BASED TOURISM IN INDIA

The strategies for development of sustainable tourism have to be formulated at two levels:

(1) A macro-level over all development strategy.

(2) Detailed micro-level strategy involving the community development.

(i) Overall Strategy for Tourism Development: The overall strategy has to include everything including the suitable legislation/guidelines, assigning responsibilities, a proper human resources development strategy including training, developing practices for community involvement, infrastructure development policy, marketing and publicity initiatives etc. It will also involve preparation of comprehensive land use plan, tourism plan, environment Impact assessment studies, environment protection measures etc.

Legislation

Formulate development strategies and guidelines, enact appropriate legislation and impose planning restrictions to ensure protection of environment, community and tourists and to ensure quality of tourist services.

Clearly define government responsibilities and create an efficient institutional structure to administer the requisite facilitation and regulatory services.

Strengthen the institutional structures, specially the Department of tourism to effectively perform the functions of planning, cooperation, project identification and implementation, development facilitation and regulatory functions.

Empower community-based institutions by providing necessary guidelines and resources by the Department of tourism. A separate 'community Unit' may be setup within the Department of tourism, to deal with community-based tourism development in the state.

Formulate and enforce comprehensive guidelines for the maintenance of tourism attractions.

Allocation of Responsibilities

Ensure that industry establishments also own the responsibility for environmental protection and community development.

Create awareness about the benefits and adverse impacts of tourism; about responsibilities of the community in protecting their own valuable assets and environment.

Human Resource Development

Evolve an effective strategy for quality Up-gradation of existing tourist accommodation, improvement of management and marketing functions of tourism industry, training of personnel and better utilization of capacities available.

Establish necessary training and quality enforcement mechanism.

Make arrangements for the training of community leaders in the management of tourism enterprises including tourism services.

Regulate the growth of tourism establishments according to clearly laid guidelines.

Strengthen tourism industry associations to facilitate product improvement, quality upgradation etc.

Community Participation

Involve the community in ensuring safety of tourists and give wide publicity to the peace process in the state and the legendary customary hospitality.

Infrastructure Development Policy

Develop infrastructure facilities in identified places and

provide incentives including training to local entrepreneurs to set up tourism facilities.

Give priority to the improvement of roads connecting tourist centers.

Give priority to the provision of basic infrastructural facilities like accommodations, preservation and maintenance of different attractions of tourism potential, ensuring availability of trained manpower in tourist centres.

Policy for Marketing and Publicity

Identify potential tourist-centers and priorities development activities at these places.

Create appropriate publicity and information materials-based on documented information that could be used for tourism promotion in identified market segments.

Establish a sound and efficient statistical system in the tourism Department of the State to develop robust statistical base for food planning tools.

Undertake market research, identify potential markets and market segments and develop specific marketing strategies with reference to each segment.

Encourage the providers of various tourist facilities to give high quality at reasonable cost so as to ensure that tourists feel they are getting their money's worth.

Documentation of Important Aspects

Take immediate steps to survey and document the oral history, flora and fauna religious and cultural aspects and other attractions of each place of tourist interest in great details. This will include art, craft, music, dance, costumes and cuisine of people.

Comprehensive Land Use and Tourism Plan for the State

Land use, tourism and infrastructure plans should be prepared to meet the long term needs for investment in these areas. These plans adopt different degrees of zoning and environmental protection. They need to tie in with the main development plan. Land use and other plans should also become a critical element of development control and need to be prepared in tandem with the officials making main developmental plan of the State including all major sectors.

It is critical that effective development control is maintained both for environmental sustainability and protection of the tourism attractions.

Protected areas need a greater degree of development control and environmental protection than other areas. For effective implementation, the long-term tourism investment program and the land use and development plan must be coordinated. Landowners and local government officials must be included in the plan preparation process, otherwise development control will lose its effectiveness and can never be enforced fully.

Good infrastructure is critically especially for those in remote areas where roads, communications and other basic facilities are likely to be poor. Government and donor agencies should therefore be involved in plan preparation and should focus upon the improvement of road links, communications, water supply and treatment, and electricity supply. Infrastructure can reduce vulnerability of population of these areas.

Environment Impact Assessment Study

Needless to say Environment Impact Assessment Study is

a must. The main components to be taken care of in any EIA are the carrying capacity, site stress and attractiveness of the area.

Carrying capacity determines the maximum number of visitors that a site can accommodate, especially during the intensive peak period use. This is to be assessed according to the desired level of protection and the ability of an area to absorb a number of people at any point of time.

Site stress measures impact level on the site taking into account its natural and ecological characteristics and measures the extent of these negative impacts and determines the need for their mitigation.

Attractiveness measures the ecological and environmental characteristics of the area that are attractive and which may change over time with an increasing intensity of tourism visits. This is a qualitative indicator.

Measurement of Socio-Culture Impact of Tourism

The measurement of the socio-culture impact of tourism, can be based on the physical numbers of visitors and the resulting impact on the local population. This should be measured by the disturbance to the working lives of local inhabitants, disturbance of the normal use of space by the local population as well as their everyday lifestyles.

Clearly this will be counter balanced by job and wealth creation/improvements in comfort and living standards. Social cost-benefit assessment can be done through surveys and interviews to access the net impact.

In case the situation demands, there are numerous ways of restricting number of visitors of which the most obvious methods is Levy of fees and charges. National park, nature reserve, or village entrance fees should be directly linked to carrying capacity. Thus, if a community considers that there are too many visitors, then these entrance fees should be very high like they are doing it in Bhutan.

Other methods of restricting visitor numbers include levying car parking charges, constraints to traffic flow, restrictions on water supply and spreading the visitor numbers over a wider area through different tour programs etc.

A situation where multiple fees are charged should be avoided. Not more than one fee should be levied in order to avoid visitor frustration. Fees should be charged on an area basis rather than levying fees for different communities. Income that is to be distributed should be agreed. The level of a management body today is taking care of interests of all stake holders.

Environment Protection Measures

It is important that the tourism attractions are protected and that long-term sustainability is an underlying theme of these projects. The community must take the ultimate responsibility for resource protection and maintenance of the environment, as it is the basis of their livelihood. For example, the community should take responsibility for rubbish clearance and environmental management. Similarly, the community could also become actively involved, in the preparation of plans and management of local traffic circulation and to monitor carrying capacity for the area. The protection of endangered species, the conservation of important buildings and the environmental protection of an attractive landscape all need the cooperation of the community, public and private sector in order for it to be effectively implemented.

Agreement for these actions and responsibilities should be reached at the partnership of stakeholders level, and implementation should be co-ordinate between all of them in the form of an action plan where each role is clearly defined. A combination of educational and environmental awareness programs are needed in order to make all members of the community aware about the need for conservation, environmental sustainability and also for identifying alternative means of income generation.

Depending on the nature of the tourism attraction, and community's desire, preference should be given to 'high value/low volume' tourism, especially in places that are sensitive in terms of social or environmental conditions. In order to effectively manage a tourism asset, and ensure its sustainable exploitation, communities must have a good understanding of that asset's tourism value and how to protect and enhance it.

Detailed Micro-Level Strategies

What are the specific issues which should be addressed in a community-based tourism project – needs to be addressed first by us before we can come to micro level strategies. **A brief list of such issues is given below:**

There is a clear need for a comprehensive community organization that is representative of all or most of the community sectors and interests.

A long-term management and advisory agency, such as an NGO, is needed to initiate maintain the project momentum.

There is also a need for a partnership organisation that assists and makes key decisions on the community-based tourism project. This organisation shall include community members, the NGOs, public sector and private sector representatives. The community must have a common vision for the sort of tourism development that it wishes to take forward, and the strategy and action.

Cohesive community leadership is essential for the proper-management of a community-based tourism initiative.

The community's values, goals and needs must be incorporated in the documents. **Community-based tourism cannot always be completely market-oriented, although attention must also be given to ensuring that the destination's tourism industry is competitive and economically sustainable.** It is critical to measure the degree of economic leakage from visitor spending patterns and to implement mechanisms or improving this in a positive manner.

It is important that the community is aware of the likely negative and positive impacts from tourism development. A 'code of conduct' is an important mitigating measure for any prospective negative social impact.

A product-market match reflecting the community's values must take a step-by-step approach that commences with the core product that is acceptable to the community and has been deleted at length by them.

Interpretation is critical in attracting specific market segments for community-based tourism destinations; If the community opts for diversifying its product-market base, the assessment of this potential should be conducted in close cooperation with the travel trade and tourism industry.

Environmental conditions, such as rubbish disposal, traffic management, pedestrian circulation, signage and interpretation must be properly managed and maintained by the community. Improvements should be funded from entrance fees and other charges; levied and collected by the community; and Community-based initiatives need to be incorporated into broader tourism networks. Villages are unlikely to be able to attract visitors in isolation, unless they are part of a layer of tourist circuit. There can be various types of community-based tourism projects.

Now we can come to the basic strategies for community-based tourism at the micro level. These are summarized as follows:

The most important strategy is to develop a representative and an efficient management organization at the community level which should be responsible for collective decision making, revenue management, distribution of revenue, management of finance etc. This organization should enforce the levying of fees to regulate number of visitors, but at the same time a avoid making it too costly to avoid visitors frustration.

The second strategy is to form a broad based partnership between community organisation/NGO/private sector and public sector. This is necessary for adding investment, infrastructure development and capital adequacy. The partnership should neither be very large and nor very small to ensure representative character along with efficiency. If there are any DONOR agencies, they should be involved in the community organisation. The NGO should be given the key driver role. The role and profit sharing of the private sector should be very clearly defined. All this should be putdown in a simple memoranda of understanding between the partners.

The third strategy is the development of small business and entrepreneurs within the community because this will not only serve tourists efficiently, but also promote poverty alleviation and growth of employment. **There should be a simple regulatory framework for business like hotels/resorts/ guides/food sellers and other traders. If the regulations are poor, it can spread the benefits equitably in the community.**

The fourth strategy is the development of skills within the community for execution of the project. In this, the community must list out the works they can do and the ones they should not do. The temptation to contracting utmost activities to outsiders should be avoided but at the same time if community members want to do some activities, they must have the required skills for which necessary training must be provided.

The fifth strategy is to avoid dependence on tourism for income. For the long term sustainability, it is important that tourism should be treated as one of the economic activities to supplement the income from other sectors. The community organisation must try to develop other activities like horticulture, floriculture, agriculture, fisheries, handicrafts etc. which will help the tourism industry, but diversify the revenue base. **The benefits of tourism must be assessed in the form of a cost benefit analysis against other economic options, so that the community doesn't suffer because of a lot of opportunity cost. It must be cleared that community-based tourism has to supplement the income and not increase risk of depending on it solely. For example if the community has extra fertile land, it may have to decide whether it will be more profitable to use that land for tourism or for additional agriculture or any other business. The community has to choose the best commercial option.**

The sixth strategy is to run the community organisation on a commercial model. Although income and employment generation as well as poverty alleviation maybe the objectives, the implementation of the project must be carried out on a commercial and competitive basis to help ensure sustainability.

Where a major tourism asset is collectively owned or controlled by the community, the management organisation needs to have good information on what price should be fixed on its access by the visitors. The pricing of access, and use of a tourism asset can normally be done on the basis of cost-recovery, where marginal cost and marginal revenue equate, **or on the basis of visitors willingness to pay.** The most important requirement in making decisions on pricing is for communities to have the best possible information about all relevant factors, especially regarding depreciation, maintenance cost, expansion costs, tourists willingness and ability to pay, competitors pricing strategies, saleable value of the asset, rentable value of the asset and marketing and promotional value of the asset.

Another strategy would be maximise revenue capture at the local land though various means, such as through constructive efforts which facilitate visitors to spend as much as possible at local level. **But the community must always remember to provide good value for money for goods and services sold to tourists.** Alternatively, the community can attempt to fulfill the needs of visitors by making available to them as many of their demanded goods and services as possible. This will require considerable coordination by local enterprises to develop necessary capabilities and supply channels. Where there is considerable visitor expenditure going to a privately-owned enterprise within a particular locality, for example home-stay accommodation, it may be appropriate to change a 'bed levy' or equivalent so that additional benefit can be spread through the community via the distribution of this.

This should be linked to administrative activities, such as directing visitors so that home-stay can prevent situations of social jealousy forming. There could be a 'community education tax' that goes directly to a school, for example. Where communities charge collective fees to tourists for admission or use of facilities, it is always desirable to be able to demonstrate transparently how those collected funds have been used, and will be used. This can often be in the form of a short information letter and will have the effect of generating some confidence among visitors that their contribution to the project, as a result of their visit, is being used appropriately for the betterment of the environment and the people.

Another strategy is to provide security of land tenure which is important for attracting investment. Security of land tenure is important for attracting investment. Land rights need to be clarified when attracting investment. In this respect, partnership mechanisms and government support are also critical. Government agencies should consider providing land for partnership and control by local communities in order to help manage tourism resources protecting environment. This will enable communities to have a greater say in their local plan preparations. It should be remembered that this aspect represents a real source of power and control for the community and should not be wasted.

The strategy of recycling and reinvesting profits in community-based tourism, is important so that real benefits are experienced on a community-wide basis. Profits should be reinvested into brining improvements to tourism products and for conservation purpose and this needs to be done on a long-term basis.

The strategies of proper human resources development and capacity building, are very important for small business, and the community organisation. They have to have-continuous training programs in place that meet the needs of skills development required by the project. The lead for this must be taken by the community organisation, preferably with support from private sector. The best approach to training for small business in communities is to adopt a long term, incremental approach, gradually incorporating new skill and knowledge, rather than trainees taking high-intensity and short-term courses. On-the-job training is often effective for the development of many skills. The implications for the community labour market need to be considered. If the community is remote, and there is low labour mobility between regions, it is possible that a community-based tourism project could overwhelm the local market for labour and so adversely affect other local industries. In all likelihood this would be just a temporary effect, but the possibility needs to be considered nonetheless.

It is also important to select the right people in the community to do the appropriate jobs. Thus, better-educated members of the community should be assigned managerial tasks. The most deprived groups must be involved, they should be appointed to positions that best suit their skills. Subsequently, training and work development can lead to their development towards taking up managerial positions. If the skills do not exist in the community then help needs to be obtained from elsewhere, such as from NGOs the private sector and donor agencies. Similarly, if there is a shortage of local manual labour, then workers will need to be brought in from other areas. This will clearly increase economic leakage, although as long as the workforce is even marginally more productive, then that leakage will probably be acceptable as long as there is some extra income generation for the community.

It is also important that staff be recruited locally, especially when it comes to unskilled work. Recruitment should be done in an equitable, just and transparent manner. Targets should be set for increasing the proportion of staff and/or locally-earned wages for communities located within 20 kms of the community-based tourism project.

Where the use of local employment is not possible or desirable, especially where more technical or managerial skills are required, then clear and transparent decisions need to be made as to why this has to be brought in from outside. The import of skills and labour should also be coupled with concurrent efforts to include on-the-job and formal training in order to allow local workers to strengthen this capacity over time and then replace the imported labour where it is efficient to do so. A variety of training and awareness programs are needed including workshops, training courses and direct experience. Training modules administered through institutions delivering accredited, appropriate courses could also be a potential source of niche training for local people. Educational and environmental awareness programs are critical to changing the local community mindset for short-term environmentally unsustainable benefits to longer term sustainable and tourism-related benefits. Intensive training and facilitation is required to allow a community to undergo organisational strengthening and institutional development. As long as the 'community structure' could manage 'community resources' there is a long-term basis.

Furthermore, outside intervention can only help to resolve internal community disputes or conflicts. The organisation of training sessions should involve local governments, relevant private sector associations, international organisations, and NGOs.

This was just an overview of the opportunities lying galore in the field of Indian Tourism wherein I just wanted to analyse the core concept of sustainability and dwell upon in detail as to how to build that into our strategy of developing our tourist infrastructure, processes and products so that they last long term and if feasible for ever. On other aspects of tourism like destinations, carrying capacity and tour travel guides, these are hundreds of publications available in the market. But we should not talk of sustainability just because of 'West' is emphasis on it, we should adopt it as a way of life and growth because of our own self interest for survival.

❏

NORTH-EAST – AN OPPORTUNITY

The Eight states of North-Eastern Region of the country represent a mix of ethnic and cultural diversity and a major constraint for their development has been their geographical isolation. In fact, before partition in 1947, isolation was lesser because of the industrial communication links through inland waterways. As of today the communication link is only through a small stretch of land called 'Siliguri Corridor'. But that notwithstanding we cannot keep such a large region of the country undeveloped. The large chunk of land mass called North-East has tremendous potential for development because of the rich natural resources including hydrocarbons and bio-diversity of its flora and fauna. There is a huge scope for food processing industry because of suitability for horticulture and plantations. It is not that Government of India has not given packages of fiscal and credit incentives for development of industry and services, but none of this would work without huge investment in infrastructure. Besides, these; North-East also has great potential for hydro electric power and tourism sector. Because of higher literacy rate (especially female literacy), there is also a scope for service industries like hospitality, airlines, medical, IT etc. North East can also act as gateway to our neighbouring countries like Myanmar, China and ASEAN countries. This will require greater and rapid connectivity with these countries. There is need for trans Asian highway, a rail link from North East to Myanmar and ASEAN Countries. There is also huge scope for inland waterways in the region. This is just a brief macro view of what can happen!

The foremost requirement for development of North-East Region is connectivity of the region within and also with the rest of the country and other countries through better rail, road, air and water transport linkages. Air journeys must be upgraded to cheap ticket options, frequency should be increased and smaller efficient aircrafts to be introduced. The mega power projects should be replaced with smaller hydel power projects because otherwise we will never have the development of estimated potential of 60,000 MW of power in North East Region. There is also need to do something serious about transmission and distribution of power within North East Region, because otherwise people of North East Region will never benefit from power availability. The lack of power also helps insurgency in an indirect way. Alongwith provision of electricity, there is need to provide excellent healthcare and education facilities in North East Region. There is need to look at small absorptive capacity of North East for large projects because local contractors do not have much capacity. Their capital base is low. They do not have equipment and expertise to carry out large projects. The State Public Works Departments are ill equipped, so solution lies in inviting big national/international companies to go into North East Region and form joint ventures with smaller local companies to do the projects there, otherwise road construction and power projects will always remain a dream! Furthermore, because there is poor road and rail network; the river waterways need to be developed. Brahmaputra and Barak rivers have huge potential.

But even smaller rivers can be inter-connected. There is urgent need to put large investments in plantations, irrigation, horticulture, handicrafts and flood control of North East Region. The region is highly prone to natural disasters like earthquake and land sliding, so there is huge need for proper town planning and disaster management which is not happening. There is also need for employment led growth in the region with a focus on local people and resources otherwise the feeder stock for insurgency will keep growing.

The unique opportunities of North East Region are in handicrafts and handloom products which can be used both for domestic and international markets. Developing entrepreneurship and creating marketing linkages are main needs of the hour. The main hurdle in North East Region is poor access to market credit and technology. Cluster approach could be one solution. The Special Economic Zones have not succeeded anywhere for reasons best known to all of us. But there is a great need for a special North East economic and exports processing zone which can facilitate trade to neighbouring countries.

Furthermore, the educational base needs to be strengthened alongwith strengthening vocation based training through ITI's and other institutions. The recently taken up initiative by Government of India for Skill Development is going to boost this in a big way. The position of women being very good in the societies of North Eastern States and communities being well knit there is great scope for 'self-help groups' to work in the region for livelihoods creation.

There is another serious problem. There is strong perception in the minds of rest of India about North East being unsafe place which deters all companies and entrepreneurs from outside to venture into North East Region for business. There is a felt, need to develop positive image of North East through media and promote North East Region as an attractive destination which needs to be explored by rest of India. We also need to market the North East Region abroad and make tourism access easier. There is a need to introduce North East history and its unique customs etc. in our school and college curricula so as to create an awareness in minds of Indian citizens. There is a need for graduating from doling out grants to building up of capacity and creation of infrastructure for North East Region.

For re-tuning the education system of North East region there is need for teacher training. Special training modules need to be developed for upgradation of skills for teachers at all levels. We need to adopt cluster approach for upgrading existing educational institutions. The centre of excellence can then be developed at some levels. These centres can be accessed by all North East Region institutions for which IT links provide the viability.

As earlier discussed in another chapter, the forte of North East Tourism is eco-tourism, adventure tourism, heritage tourism and religious tourism. Tourist footfalls are very little because the tourists are visiting mainly Assam, Sikkim and Meghalaya. The main issue hampering the development of tourism is not only the lack of basic infrastructure but it also has to tackle the security perception, inadequate community participation and lack of private sector initiative. The Gangtok Declaration on Tourism and the Hospitality Sector in 2007 which was announced in the Fourth Sectoral Summit of North Eastern Council had said that,

"The Tourism sector holds the highest promise for generating large employment and income-augmentation opportunities spreading and reaching down to all segments of society in all States of the North-East Region (NER). Capital costs are modest compared to large industrial investments and gestation periods are short. Moreover, as is being recognized by the hospitality industry all over India, the people of North-East are exceptionally well-endowed, in terms of personal and social characteristics and a long tradition of hospitality in their homes and communities, for employment in the hospitality industry. Therefore, the tourism sector should be e thrust area for NEC intervention during the Eleventh Plan Period. State governments in NER must take full advantage of Ministry of Tourism schemes and NEC/NCLPR funding for tourism development and promotion, especially for infrastructure related to the tourism and the hospitality sector. To this end, State governments must prioritizetourism, including addressing priority issues such as making land available, upgrading expertise to prepare project proposals and minimizing delays in implementing projects. The involvement of communities through panchayats and village development boards, as also of the private sector, is of the essence for the development of the tourism and the hospitality industry.

The single most inhibiting factor is the perception of NER is being ridden with insurgency, militancy and terrorism. This perception is so much at variance with ground realities that projecting a true and nuanced picture of the vast swathes in NER of total peace and tranquility, impeccable law and order, and iron-clad security for the tourism is as essential for the development and promotion of tourism in NER as for investment in other sectors of development.

Poor connectivity has been a major impediment to the development of tourism in NER. But there is now a concerted drive to rapidly augment all kinds of connectivity within NER and between NER and the rest of India, as well as the world at large, particularly South-East Asia. The Government of India will be investing about ₹ 50,000 crore on the construction of road and highways in the North-East in the next five years. The rail network is being substantially augmented. National waterway-II (the Brahmaputra River) will shortly be made fully operational from Sadiya to Dhubri and the Barak River is expected to be shortly declared as National Waterway-VI. The Kolodyne River through Mizoram and up to Sittwe in Myanmmar is being developed. Already, the density of civil airports in NER is the highest in India and recent GOI policies had led to about 226 flights a week between NER and the rest of the country. Intra-region connectivity is now the watchword and plans are in hand to reach a target of nearly 600 flights a week within the region during the first half of the Eleventh Plan period. There is, moreover, a new emphasis on power generation which is expected to render NER surplus in power during the current Eleventh Plan period. Every effort will be made to ensure that transmission and distribution systems are directed toward 'Power to the People'.

It is particularly significant to note that hotels (two-star category and above), and adventure and leisure sports, including ropeways, have been included in the new North-East Industrial and Investment Promotion Policy, 2007 (NEIIPP) effective 1.4.2007 which has extended fiscal incentives to the service sector. Not only has the hospitality sector thus been rendered virtually tax-free but also eligible for generous capital subsidies and interest subsidies. Detailed notifications under the NEIIPP, 2007 would be notified by the Department of Industrial Promotion and Policy, hopefully within the next few weeks.

In the same conference many decisions were taken listed as below. Some of these have been acted upon and rest are still awaiting implementation by various stakeholders.

(i) The target groups for tourism promotion are both domestic and foreign tourist, with the highest priority being accorded to the domestic sector and particularly targeted at States like Gujarat and West Bengal which generate a high proportion of domestic tourism. It is also important to target potential segments of society such as government servants holidaying on Leave Travel Concessions (LTC).

(ii) Tourism in NER should be constructed around four concentric circles:

(a) Multi-State tourism circuits. (Given the geographical location of Sikkim, it may develop, in the first instance, multi-State links with West Bengal, particularly the Darjeeling Gorkha Hills Area).

(b) Pan regional tourism involving the development of linkages within NER and between NER and other regions of the country, particularly the eastern region.

(c) International tourism with connectivity from within NER to neighboring and other foreign countries. For the promotion of international tourism, it has to be recognized and promoted that South-East Asia begins in North-East India.

(iii) At an all India level, the small domestic tourist traffic has increased from 250 million to 400 million, of which foreign tourist traffic is estimated at no more than 2 to 3 million per annum. This requires that the thrust of NER tourism development should be on domestic tourist, while, of course, also tapping into the international traffic.

(iv) Bengalese and Gujaratis are known to be a great travelers; hence they should be the target of promotional efforts.

(v) To promote tourism, relaxation and liberalization of the ILP/RAP/PAP regimes should be undertaken on a State-wise basis in consultation with the States concerned.

(vi) For attracting domestic tourists, the emphasis should be on developing Dharamshalas, one room accommodation, low costs/low budget hotels, youth hostels and accommodations along rivers and near centuries."

There was another Sectoral Summit of North Eastern Council which had reviewed the air connectivity and its Aizwal declaration in 2007 said,

"Most of the places in the North Eastern Region are inaccessible and located in far-flung areas. The road and rail infrastructure in inadequate, therefore, air connectivity is the most viable means of transportation in the Region both for intra-State connectivity and the Region's linkage to the mainland."

There are a total of 23 airports in the North Eastern Region out of which 11 are operational. These airports are – Agartala, Aizwal, Dibrugarh, Dimapur, Guwahati, Imphal, Jorhat, Lilabari, Shillong, Silchar and Tezpur. The airport at Lengpui, Aizwal is owned by the State Govt. The 12 non-operational airports are – Along, Daparizo, Kailashahar, Kamalpur, Khowai, Pasighat, Rupsi, Tezu, Tura, Turial, Zrio and Shella.

Three proposed Greenfield airpots are to be developed at Itanagar, Cheithu and Pakyong. Two new Greenfield airports have been proposed at Tawang and Kokrajhar. Category-I routes are having 12 major trunk-routes. Category-II routes are stations in NE Region, J&K, Andaman and Nicobar and Lakshadweep, scheduled operators have to deploy 1% of capacity deployed on Category-I routes. For Category-III routes which are route other than in the categories mentioned, scheduled operators have to deploy 50% of capacity deployed on Category-I routes.

It is noticed that all the airlines operating in Category-I routes have fulfilled the requirement as per DGCA Route Dispersal Guidelines. The airlines operating in the Region have been Indian Airlines, Alliance Air, Jet Airways, Air Deccan, Kingfisher Airlines, Spicejet, Air Sahara and Indigo etc. There has been an increase in capacity, both with regard to flights per week and seats deployed. Besides aircraft operations, helicopter services also operate in the NE Region. Pawan Hans Helicopters Ltd. have deployed various categories of helicopters in four States of NER which include one helicopter each in Meghalaya, Tripura, Sikkim and Arunachal Pradesh. Besides these Jagson Airlines has deployed one helicopter in Arunachal Pradesh. There is one helicopter in Arunachal Pradesh. There is one Dauphin helicopter of Pawan Hans which is in lease to MHA for operational requirements.

A number of major works were completed during last two Plan Periods at various airports in the North Eastern Region. This included construction of new terminal building at Agartala and Lilabari; upgradation of terminal building at Guwahati; strengthening and extension of runway for AB-320 operations was carried out at Dimapur, Agartala, Imphal and Lilabari.

Night landing operations are currently possible only at few airports like Agartala and Guwahati etc. It is expected that night operations will be possible at many more airports soon. Instrument Landing Systems (ILS) are in place at Agartala, Dibrugarh, Dimapur, Guwahati and Imphal. Various projects involving installation of navigational equipment such as Communication, Navigation and Surveillance (CNS), Doppler Very High Frequency Range (DVOR), Digital Satellite Communication Network (DSCN), Digital Automatic Terminal Information Service (DATIS), Digital Video Tape Recorder (DVTR) have been on-going in various airports of the Region.

For various upgradation works to be carried out in some airports there are problems of land acquisition.

H.E. Governor of Manipur, Dr. S.S. Sidhu gave a detailed presentation of the study on a 'Dedicated Airline for the North Eastern Region' undertaken by the Committee chaired by him. The study indicated the following points for consideration:

- The dedicated airline should be based in North East and its operations dedicated to the Region.
- The operations should function as a hub and spoke model with the initial hub at Guwahati and sub-hub to be established at Imphal and Agartala.
- The type of aircraft should be Short Haul, Short Take-Off and Landing (STOL), Turbo-prop with a seating capacity of 15 to 20.
- The public notice for Expression of Interest to be issued at the earliest.
- Technical and financial bids to be called from short-listed entities.
- Finalization of entity/operator for dedicated operations in the NER.
- Representative from Tripura did not commit on the decision to go for a dedicated airlines for the North

Eastern Region. He sought time to confirm his State Government's position in this regard.
- Representative from Sikkim stated that Bagdogra should continue to be an airport within the ambit of the dedicated airlines till such time the airport at Pakyong was developed.
- Alliance Air indicated that the main reason for its erratic services was shortage of pilots which has now been overcome. They also confirmed that the ATR services (four aircrafts) is being strictly being implemented within the North Eastern Region.
- Alliance Air indicated that they are committed to improving the services in the Region and are willing to insert an effective Penalty Clause in case the services were not upto expectations.
- The dedicated airline should operate under the 'Bush Operations' concept where the small aircraft will hop from location to location. The airports so serviced should include the small airports which need to be operationalized."

The detailed recommendations above show very clearly the status of connectivity, solutions available and what needs to be done.

Furthermore, there were many other summits of the North-Eastern Council. The Sixth Summit of 2007 was on rail connectivity and it had issued a Delhi Statement of Rail Connectivity in the North East Region. Another North-Eastern Council Summit on IT-enable Services and Telecommunications had issued its Kohima declaration. The Eighth Sectoral Summit of North East Summit was on HRD Sector and had also given conclusions in the sector. The Eighth Sectoral Summit was on

Sports, Art and Culture and had also given some important suggestions.

The Third Sectoral Summit on Inland Water Transport had highlighted the issues and conclusions about Inland Water Transport as below. It said

"that Inland Water Transport offers a shorter and cheaper route for transport of bulk commodities and project cargo. It is operational even during flood season and offers large employment potential, therefore, development of IWT in NER is a strategic and economic imperative."

Need for increasing investments and increasing efficiency of IWT mode was recognized by the Conference. The Brahamaputra River had already been declared as a national waterway and for river Barak the process was on. RITES was doing a feasibility study for river Kaladan in Mizoram for multi-mode transport.

There is a need for river conservation works, maintenance of floating terminals, construction of cargo handling facilities. There is need to carry out feasibility studies for various river projects and to create awareness among people to use waterways.

There is also a need to build up long term protocols on IWT with neighbouring countries as a part of look east or act east policy of the Government of India and also to develop credible night navigation facilities on national waterways to reduce travel time. Our officers need to be trained abroad for studying such facilities. There is a need is enable mechanical handling of cargo instead of manual handling. The funding requirements have to be met by Ministry of Shipping/IWAI/ Ministry of DONER who should converge their schemes for this one purpose.

There have been some other Summits on Floods and Erosion Control programme, on plantation crops and on and road sector. The Shillong Statement on Roads and Highways provides a very interesting study. It highlights the issue like this.

"Road connectivity in the North-East Region is well below the national average on most parameters. Therefore, extending, intensifying and improving the roads network is essential to economic development of the region and welfare of its people."

The high priority to be accorded to the development of roads in the North-East Region is well reflected in the Union Government's intention to invest huge amounts on the roads sector in the North-East. There has been a 16-fold increase in the physical quantity of road works being undertaken, compared to past period. However, in view of the variety of roads involved and the multiplicity of agencies concerned, it was felt that there was a need to pull together all diverse elements of road development programme into a single Master Plan for the Region.

There was pressing need to exponentially increase the absorptive capacity of States of North-East Region to ensure implementation of ambitious plans for road development. This calls for putting in place a back-up human resources infrastructure programme for capacity building and training of State PWDs and RWDs and other state agencies concerned, as well as contractors, especially those based in the region There was a need to train them in preparing project proposals and Detailed Project Reports (DPRs); preparation and processing of tender documents; also supervision of execution of contracts to ensure quality specifications and management and maintenance of road sector assets after completion of works.

The eight States of the North-East Region feel they do not have adequate budgetary resources of their own to handle maintenance responsibilities which devolve on them after roads are built, an obligation that will exponentially increase with significant increase in road sector activity envisaged. The initiative taken by Mizoram to establish through legislation a 'Roads Maintenance Fund' is commended for emulation by other North-Eastern States.

With a view to equipping NER-based contractors with machinery and equipment to participate in larger numbers or more effectively and efficiently in the huge road building programme. There is a need to establish depots at appropriate locations in the North-East from where contractors might hire their requirements of equipment/machinery to meet very large demand to implement road network development programme.

There is a need for state government of eight NER States to realise that there are some problems which only they can solve; like land acquisition, forest issues, encroachments and providing security to outside contractors.

There was a high level task force of connectivity and promotion of trade and investment in North Eastern States which had made recommendations to develop infrastructure and create other enabling conditions in NE Region, which seem to have prime deterring effect on investment in the region.

There is a need to provide better incentives under the North East Industrial Policy than those being offered under the industrial policies for the states of Uttaranchal/Himachal Pradesh/J&K. There is also a need to promote industrial development based on natural resources of the region like hydro power, gas, bamboo, horticulture.

It will be even if states of the Region, under the aegis of NEC, come together for evolving a comprehensive regional industrial policy so as to make NER a single Economic Unit through removal of internal barriers, uniform taxation regime and by promoting NE brand equity.

There is a need to strengthen public sector institutions, such as NERAMAC, NEHHDC and NEDFi, transfer in joint ventures (with majority private ownership) and make these proactive to provide professional guidance and support to entrepreneurs. Also we need to accelerate the activities of various commodity boards for Tea, Coffee, Spices etc. in the Region. We need to enable NEDFi to play a substantial role in the development of NER.

We can adopt Mission approach for specific areas of Industrial growth such as bamboo processing, horticulture produce processing and for use of medicinal and aromatic resources. We can pursue growth of IT sector vigorously and develop IT parks to utilize literate and educated manpower. This industry is not dependent on transportation networks and raw material supply. We can also incentivize service sectors, Power generation, Bio technology, Tourism related activities, Hospital and Nursing homes and Vocational training institutes. Since handloom industry is traditional to the Region, evolve a special policy for development of the handloom sector with linkages with the contemporary markets, design, etc. especially for exports.

We can open new ITIs and strengthen existing ones, better faculty and equipments to provide for market-driven high skills in their trainees.

We can Promote vigorously NER as an attractive destination for investment through persistent image building and holding of NER Business Summits. For improving border trade we can improve and construct all weather Highways, RCC Bridges etc., leading to 12 major Land Customs Stations (LCSs).

We can use Karimganj-Sylhet-Dhaka Road for Transportation, extend Amguri-Mokochung-Tuensang Road linking Myanmar. We can do the construction of road from Indo-Myanmar border to NH-54 at Nalkawn (Mizoram) to provide Kaladan multi-modal transport. We can do the up-gradation of NH-39 and 53 connecting Indo-Myanmar Border Via Dimapur and Silchar. We need to do connection of North-East to Trans Asian Highways. We need to do construction on priority basis of 1300 KM long trilateral Highway connecting Moreh (India), Bagan (Myanmar) and Maesot (Thailand). We can also provide the bus service between Guwahati-Imphal-Mandley, Guwahati-Dhaka via Shillong and Guwahati-Tura-Dhaka to facilitate movement of the business community.

We can also restore Mohisashan (Assam, India)-Shahbazpur (Bangladesh) railway traffic to facilitate export of bulk mineral (coal, limestone), food items and agro-horticulture based products from NER. There is a need to double track the Railway line from new Jalpaiguri to Tinsukia via Dimapur. We can connect NE with Trans Asian Railways for faster movement of goods.

We can create an air travel circuit between North East and Bhutan, Nepal, Bangladesh, Myanmar, China, Thailand, Singapore to increase Export and Tourism from the region. We can also provide an Air Cargo Complex at LGB Airport, Guwahati to cater to Export and Import of goods. We need to construct Integrated Export Complex including Customs Office, Immigration, Banking, Clearing and Forwarding Agents buildings, Truck parking bay, Warehouses, Cold Storage Facilities, Post Offices, Telephone Exchange, Shopping Centres, BSF Complex, Police Outpost, Electronic Weigh Bridges, Electricity, Potable Drinking Water, Health Facility etc. at all the

12 notified LCSs. We should develop Border Towns and Trade Centres at major LCSs of NER. We should also open more border trading points with adequate infrastructural facilities and upgrading the infrastructure at non-functional LCS of the region and create more border haats and regularize these haats.

No border trade can happen without adequate banking. Banks functioning in NER should have correspondent arrangements with Banks in the neighbouring countries. At present this correspondent relationship are restricted to the Banks functioning in Kolkata. We should install high value currency chests at major towns near LCSs. We should also regularize and institutionalize Letter of Credit (L/C) arrangement between the Banks of India and Myanmar for smooth and enhanced border trade through Moreh and Zokhawthar.

We need to pursue with Bangladesh to reduce Tariffs. North East exports to Bangladesh suffer High Tariff Barriers since the Customs duty structure in Bangladesh includes Value Added Tax, Advance Income Tax and Infrastructure Development Charge in addition to Basic Customs Duty. We should also pursue neighbouring countries for duty free import/export.

We should persuade neighbouring countries to open their visa offices in the North East. Ensuring more exchange of trade delegations and Buyer – seller meets, Exhibition of goods at regular intervals with neighbouring countries will also be helpful.

The creation of infrastructure for development of export from the region and co-ordinate export promotion efforts in this region with various Union Ministries should be done by NEC. NE states should bring exports in their development agenda and improve law and order at LCS and enroute. We need to develop brand image for special products of NE for export enhancement. We also should create and constantly update interactive website for NER to facilitate border trade. We should also set-up a branch of Indian Institute of Foreign Trade in North East for development of professional manpower and creation of entrepreneurship in Foreign Trade. There are only few steps which have been indicated in conferences but it is not an exhaustive list.

On the power front, considering low density of the population in NE states, local demand would be better served with smaller projects feeding independent local grids, minimizing T&D costs and logistic problems.

Arunachal has already decided not to encourage projects involving large storage as there are very few suitable sites for construction of multipurpose storage projects. For North-East we should identify zone for easily implementable projects in a single region to reduce both infrastructure and transmission costs. We need to undertake Survey and Investigation of HE Projects through experienced hydro-power developers to minimize the geological uncertainties during construction. Electronically operated Theodolite Survey Machines (EDM) along with lightweight drilling machines need to be used for geological surveys. Global Positioning System (GPS) also to be provided. We need to convert identified Meter gauge to Broad Gauge rail links and extend rail network, develop adequate road network and strengthen existing roads along with construction of bridges, air services, effective tele-communication for smooth implementation of identified HE projects. This is already being done but needs to be fast tracked.

We need to build high capacity lines for evacuation of power from various HEPs. Devise modalities for commitment to pay transmission charges accordingly. It would be desirable to adopt the national approach in which beneficiaries outside NER share the transmission charges of identified transmission system in NER based on power allocation from NER generation projects.

We may strengthen transmission and distribution system to provide uninterrupted power supply particularly to industrial Areas. New Sub-transmission and adequate distribution infrastructure through APDRP would be of great help. We may bring about greater competition in creation of transmission assets, increase debt component and move to competitive bidding to reduce transmission charges in NER.

North Eastern Region has a Vision 2020 document which was a collective effort of numerous intellectuals and institutions, organisations and public personnel and all the governments of the North East alongwith Ministry of Development on Northern Eastern Region had noted in its content that:

"Inclusive growth calls for inclusive governance. The North Eastern Region has long-established traditions of community-based economic and social organisation. This has facilitated a smooth transition to contemporary institutions of Pachayati Raj in all of Sikkim and Arunachal Pradesh; most of Assam and Tripura; and the valley areas of Manipur. The States of Meghalaya and Mizoram in their entirety and certain parts of Assam and Tripura fall under the Sixth Schedule of the Constitution and the institutions of local governance established there under for these areas, reinforced by village level administration and development through village councils and village development boards respectively, set up as per Naga customary practices and usages, and also duly mandated

by the State's Acts and Rules. The Nagaland experience of Communitization has been help up as the exemplar for the country as a whole by none less than former President Abdul Kalam. Thus the North Eastern Region is well-equipped with institutions of inclusive governance to assure inclusive growth. This Vision for accelerated and inclusive growth is predicted on the growth process involving and spreading through these various institutions of democratic, representative, participative and popular development. They also said inclusive growth calls for attention to inclusive governance and rural development. The single biggest constraint to accelerated growth is poor infrastructure affecting:
— road connectivity
— rail connectivity
— air connectivity
— cyber and telecom connectivity
— inland waterways
— power"

The document noted that Human resources are the single most promising development asset of the North East. A talented people, with standards of literacy well above the national average, their potential is being stifled by inadequate access to quality education, vocational education, training in languages (including Hindi, English and foreign languages), training in computers and IT, technical training, and business and management skills. Investment in education and sports, arts and culture, and capacity-building in general, is a soft investment with enormous potential for high economic returns. A concerted effort to create centres of excellence (like IITs/IIITs/IIMs) through both public and private initiatives is essential to address the critical skill shortages, especially in higher and technical education for the region. Each State should have at least one such centre. With 96 per cent of the borders of the North Eastern Region constituting international boundaries, and in explicit recognition of the need to break the fetters of the geo-political isolation of the region, it is necessary to factor in what the Minister of External Affairs has described as 'new inputs' in foreign, defence, internal security and international trade policy. To this end, the immediate priority is to build the required infrastructure right up to the border areas, establishing connectivity and communication links to the cross-border points through which trade and economic exchanges with the countries neighbouring the North Eastern Region are proposed to be promoted under the Look East Policy. This priority is to be accorded by all Central agencies concerned and State Governments because while the Look East Policy has yielded few returns to the Region thus far, it is in North East India and South-East Asia begins and, as such, it is for the North East to be enable to play the arrow-healed role in the further evolution of this Policy. This requires a redefining of the Look East Policy to resolve outstanding issues of trade, transit and investment with the countries neighbouring the region. It also involves promoting Indian investment in infrastructure in partner countries, especially Myanmar, particularly in respect of ports such as Sittwe and international highways to connect the North Eastern Region to ASEAN.

Such investment might also be encouraged where required for transit between the Region to ASEAN. Such investment might also be encouraged where required for transit between the Region and the rest of India, as also for trade with the neighbourhood and beyond. However, in such a process, we recognize that it is critical to address the challenges of border management, especially with regard to cross border migration, terrorism, drugs and arms supply and other forms of non-conventional security threats for ensuring the rights and traditions of local ethnic groups comprehensively in the context of global forces of change.

The document concluded that to significantly narrow, let alone eliminate within the next decade or so, the growing gap between growth rates in the country as a whole and much of the North Eastern Region calls for a massive increase in the flow of financial resources to the Region, exponentially much large than the current or presently envisaged flow. However, the investment required would more than pay for itself over a relatively short period of time as the Region is abundantly endowed with natural and human resources that would almost immediately, and certainly within a brief gestation period, start contributing to the overall growth of the national economy, instead of, as at present, dragging down the country's overall economic performance. With tightly set targets, clear outcomes, strategies, and coordinated planning for the Region as a whole, the North East can be revitalized to become increasingly self-sufficient and a net positive contributor to the national exchequer and the country's economy. Initiating the process is the imperative requirement.

It also noted that there are three critical non-economic requirements that will condition economic performance on the ground:
— Law and order, especially internal security
— Good governance, including governance at the grassroots through institutions of local self-government.
— Diplomatic initiatives with the neighbourhood of the North East to secure what the Minister of External

Affairs has described as the 'new paradigm' where "foreign policy initiatives lend seamlessly with our national economic development requirements".

The intricate cultural and ethnic mosaic which the North-East region represents, with over 200 ethnic groups with their own languages and socio-cultural identity, coupled with factors such as geographical location and connectivity, poses a variety of challenged on the law and order and security fronts. The extensive international borders of various States in the region, while offering opportunities in the context of the 'Look East Policy', also add further complexity to the security situation. This is further compounded by the regional aspirations of the different groups in various States, a number of whom have taken up arms and have been indulging in violence. Keeping all this in view, although law and order is constitutionally the responsibility of the State Governments, the Ministry of Home Affairs, in close coordination following an integrated and multi-faceted strategy, including supplementing the efforts and resources of the State Governments to strengthen their security related arrangements, dialogue with groups who have shown a willingness to unconditionally abjure violence and come into mainstream, discussions at the diplomatic level in respect of security related matters, strengthening the arrangements for border management including infrastructural and human resource development in the border areas. Efforts are being made on a continuing basis to fine tune the various elements of the strategy as may be required, from time to time, keeping in view the special needs of different areas and people in region.

Good governance calls for probity, transparency and accountability. This is a matter of both ethics and governance systems. Effective devolution, reinforced by social audit, will considerably strengthen monitoring and vigilance at the grassroots level and, hopefully, gradually impact higher echelons of governance. Equally, the importance of capacity-building and institution-building cannot be over-emphasized. It is no longer the availability of financial resources but the capacity of institutions and individuals in the North East to make effective use of available resources that is proving the critical constraint to growth. To combat this, every effort needs to be made to induct good officers from all over the country, as well as from within the North Eastern Region, into all levels of governance. Institution-building calls for strengthening State departments and agencies, as well as promoting fruitful partnerships between civil society and State Governments. Strengthening of institutions of local self-government is particularly important. At the regional and national level, the North Eastern Council and the Ministry of Development of North Eastern Region need to be re-conceived and fully equipped, in terms of duns and personnel, to meet the challenges of implementing North Eastern Region Vision 2020. Regional institutions under the aegis of the North Eastern Council such and NERIWALM and others like NEDFI and NERAMAC, require restructuring, revamping and rejuvenation.

India's Look East Policy was developed and enacted during the government of Prime Minister Shri P.V. Narasimha Rao and was rigorously followed by successive administrations of A.B. Vajpayee and Dr. Manmohan Singh. India's strategy has focused on forging close economic and commercial ties, increasing strategic and security co-operation and the emphasis on historic cultural and ideological links with the countries in Southeast Asia. India seeks to create and expand regional markets for trade, investments and industrial development.

North eastern region has also gained prominence in the diplomatic initiatives with our neighbouring countries and the foreign policy under India's Look East policy. The region is now considered India's gate way to Southeast and East Asia.

The North-Eastern states have evinced keen interest in the BCIM initiative. Bangladesh, India, China and Myanmar-Economic corridor (BCIM-EC) is a sub regional grouping that seeks to deepen friendly cooperation among the four member nations and linking south Asia with Southeast and East Asia by building multi-model connectivity, harnessing economic complementarities and enhancing people to people relations. The primary focus of the corridor is to facilitate trade and connectivity between the landlocked and underdeveloped South-Western parts of china and the North-Eastern region of India. The proposed corridor may originate from Kunming in china and pass though Yangon and Mandalay in Myanmar, Chittagong-Dhaka Sylhet in Bangladesh entering through North eastern states and ending in Kolkata. It would be the revival of ancient Southern Silk Routes and its south western routes.

The implementation of several ambitious projects and subsequent linking of all four countries will open up the entire North Eastern region to south East and East Asia. The region's integration with the fastest growing economies of these area will lead to the economic resurgence in these landlocked States as they have to pay a higher price for transportation.

The 'Look East Policy' should also involve the constituent states of the region as stakeholders as they can be capable of playing a role in this kind of comprehensive endeavour and the political leadership of these states may be integrated with these efforts. The Chief Ministers of two-three states of the region may be considered to be on the official delegations during the high level of exchange between India and Myanmar, or

Bangladesh, Nepal, Thailand, Vietnam, Laos, Cambodia, Japan, South Korea and Japan. They can be the best Ambassadors and their presence might prove to be a powerful force multiplier.

It is true that apart from other reasons is lack of development is also caused by insurgency and tourism in the region I have mentioned in this book elsewhere about the security perception of the area. Because of this profit seeking private investment does not want to come into North East Region. Therefore, public investment has to play a more broad active role in North East Region. Infrastructure like road, bridges, railways, power generation, proper drainage and waste disposal, flood control, irrigation, drinking water, hotels and transport, airports have to be the most urgent priority. There is also need for increasing income generating potential. The role of the States shall be to ensure basic minimum need like the mobility of goods and services within the Region and outside the Region, Law and order and peace alongwith ease of doing business. The Government of India has already gone ahead with the major paragonship by signing the peace accord with the insurgent groups in last one month which may be a beginning of baby steps towards creation of peace in the Region.

I can say on the basis of my 20 years of service in the North Eastern Region that huge potential of power generation by hydro projects can solve the power issues of the whole country. The development of North East is must for generating employment opportunities and tackling the problem of insurgency. May be we should think in terms of a North East hydel commission for coordinating activities relating to developing of hydro electric potential of North East with full participation of all North East states.

Regarding tourism we can learn from China example. For example, the regions like Tibet, Xinxiang opened to tourism in eighties and used age old legacy of Silk Route for Xinxiang and the Shangri-La mystique for Buddhist Tibet. Both these regions are doing extremely well as far as tourism activities are concerned. It is a question of proper marketing. Since then the other regions of China like Mangolia and Yunnan have been doing very well so it is not that relative isolation and difficulty of access can hinder tourism forever. China has shown the way. We can do the same.

Before outlining potential areas of trade in North-East it will be interesting to examine the special features of North-East which are reiterated as below:

All the eight NE states differ considerably from each other and do not have a common political or economic agenda. The multiplicity of states in the North-East complicates matters and does not allow for uniform policy prescriptions. Although all the NE states are small, they are characterized by a very high degree of ethnic and social diversity, which complicates politics and makes it hard to pursue balanced and uniform policies. Thanks to the high female literacy rates, women must be involved in economic development activities for these activities to succeed.

Although per capita incomes in the North-East are neither high nor low (in the US$ 200-300 range), they are not accurate indicators of the quality of life. People in the NER are much better off than those in other parts of India. This is because of the strong role of the community and other necessities. However, the same community rights which ensure that nobody dies of hunger also give an open license to people to destroy forests and other natural wealths they deem fit. This way of living also makes it difficult to opt for large-scale commercial agriculture. Statistical data pertaining to the North-East is not very reliable-all figures, especially on net/gross state domestic products and poverty rates, are by and large guesstimates (except for Assam). The North-East suffers from weak infrastructure and heavy reliance on subsistence agriculture. The monsoon is characterized by extremely heavy spells of rainfall over a short period of five months, causing severe erosion and floods, especially because of depletion of the forest cover.

The NER has underdeveloped infrastructure for industries and poor communications links. The states have small capitals and few district hubs. The region is dotted with small local markets; but there is an absence of market towns. Moreover, the North East has poor supporting services, like hotels, banking and insurance. Industries in the North-East mostly manufacture food-and wood-based products. There are very few metallic, oil and gas, jute, paper and handicrafts industries in the region. The few that exist are in the small and medium-scale sector. The only exceptions are paper-and timber-based industries. There is limited mining of coal and limestone. The isolation of the NER, with the attendant high transaction costs, is perpetuating low growth rates in the region. The a few states have experience high growth, but it has been confined to the communications sector and government services.

The North-East suffers from severe logistical handicaps. The entire region is landlocked except for Assam. The terrain is mostly hilly. A majority of the states have no airport, or have small airstrips, and no rail access. Building railway lines in the region is a high-cost proposition. Transportation is thus a huge bottleneck. Despite the high literacy rates in the region, the education system is professionals, such as accountants, architects, engineers, consultants, etc., in the North-East.

The trade potential of North East lies in the following areas:
- Fruit and vegetable processing
- Meat and poultry products
- Cereal-based products
- Consumer industry
- Milk and milk-based products
- Food packaging
- Paper products
- Jute products
- Cattle/poultry/fishery feed production
- Processing of edible oils/vanaspati
- Processing of essential oils and fragrances (medicinal and aromatic plants)
- Raising plantation crops and their processing
- Gas-based intermediate products
- Value addition to timber products
- Horticulture, especially fruits (pineapple, orange, passion fruit, plum, peach)
- Hydro-electric projects
- Adventure and eco-tourism
- Bamboo-based industries

This is an indicative list and not an exhaustive one. There could be more areas.

Why had I chosen to include North-East in the book? Because when we think of tourism/horticulture/hydropower – half the potential of India lies here and we have forgotten to utilize it, develop it. Can we allow this strategically important region to remain undeveloped? At our own period, may be; with China sitting on the other side – developing his side of North-East?

❑

LAST BUT NOT THE LEAST

Towards the end I can only say that the days of 'isms' are over as now simply rigid ideologies or philosophies do not work anymore. It is the century of knowledge and technology which dominate the world. International landscape is changing dramatically as seamless borders are being created. Russia has broken down. China has changed and has become an economic super power but even with the success of capitalism it is no more acceptable without a human face.

Even social welfare can no longer to be doled out because citizens have to be empowered to decide for themselves on what is it they actually want. In the new world, as knowledge is power, information on economy, commerce and trade is the most important factor.

And it is no longer Information Technology; it has gone beyond to Nano Technology and Clean Energy. The economy has become Bio Economy. There is talk about gene therapy and genetic engineers. **The medical profession is set to undergo a radical change, especially when the entire and complete genetic map or the genome of the complete human body becomes available. Symptomatic treatment will give place to focused causative/curative treatment, that is the cause of an illness would be clearly diagnosed and treatment prescribed, making the ordinary General Physicians or these called MBBS** doctors a redundant class. **It will become the age of the specialists to whom the patients will go directly to get treated of an ailment.**

Genetically modified crops are no longer an anathema. The future is going to be in the realm of computer enabled services. **Governments are still living in the world of complicated procedures and regulatory mind sets which will have to change for speedy governance without which it cannot deliver citizen focused services. Governance has to change radically empowering its citizens, if it wants quick development.** It is but factual that Indians globally are great, but within their own country, especially in the Government, they cannot give their best as they are trapped in the quagmire of archaic mind sets of outdated rules and procedures. It is not only that bureaucrats have to be trained, we also need to train the Ministers, Members of Parliament and legislative assemblies and judges and the lowest levels of Government which interact with the public.

Furthermore, people have to be involved in the affairs of the State. The beneficiaries have to be directly involved in development and maintaining the resources which Government allocates. The local Government needs to be strengthened removing the intermediaries, delegating all powers so that good governance takes place.

The Government needs to take consistent feedback from the grass roots and the Government needs to encourage work on innovative and futuristic ideas which will pave the way for a great nation which is the future of India as I see it.

This, in short, is the Future of India, when **mindsets change, archaic rules and regulations are thrown out of the window, authorities interact directly with the people and**

know and understand their problems so that they can quickly resolve them and futuristic ideas that visualize problems' arising out of population growth and scarce resources are all addressed to in a planned manner so that the economy becomes sustainable and every citizen is guaranteed a basic minimum standard of life with all modern facilities. The Prime Minister's clarion call to 'Make in India'/'Skill India'/'Digital India'/'Swachh Bharat' – All these are laying the foundation for inclusive development. India's core challenge lies in building a competitiveness in its industries and agriculture without creating a burden on the environment and also without compromising on the rights of the labour. Make in India alongwith Make for India can be harbinger on economic transformation and can call multiplier effect in creating jobs and maximising incomes alongwith sustainable development. There is need to be a share vision among the regulators and the developers of industry for taking the nation ahead.

Before the book was going into publication, some momentous events have taken place in the world which may not be earth shattering but may have serious implications for Indian Economy so I thought we must reflect upon them.

One such major event is Chinese economy slowing down which has caused a fall in commodity prices and de-linking of global trade from GDP growth. The collapse in commodity prices has damaged fundamentals of those emerging market economies like Russia which heavily relied on resource exports. While it may be positive for emerging economies like India but Chinese devaluation of their currency is something serious and no one is going to escape the pain to be caused because of this. It will affect in the short term all assert classes all over the world. Even India will not be spared the pain and there will be outflows of foreign capital from our country as well.

What led to the great fall of China? Let us understand in flashback. The real estate curbs in China and government measures to boost stock markets led to boom of 2014. Chinese masses bought billions work of stocks. The stock markets of China almost doubled. Since buying was financed by borrowing, the bubble burst after six months wiping out $650 billion from Chinese markets. Chinese government trying to prop up market from outside did not help Chinese markets almost fell more than 30 percent in six months. The stock market burst does not mean Chinese economy is in permanent crisis but it does mean that engine is slowing down and their growth model is out of steam. Chinese melt down while being an adversity in short term is also an opportunity for India. But it will be a mistake to assume that Chinese economy is collapsing. Not, it is not. They are just changing gear. They are shifting from excessive reliance on manufacturing to services sector and consumer goods and they are doing it successfully. Rebalancing will take time but they will do it, rest assured. So instead of gloating over their fall, and waiting for bonanza of FDI to fall in your lap, it will be better if our country puts its act together and gets done with structural reforms in next one year or we would have missed this thin window of opportunity also.

India has a unique opportunity to reposition itself as a country which is better than China for doing business but this cannot happen if our country does not get its house in order. Now, let us come to our advantages. We are saving to the extent of ₹ 20,000 crore per annum on account of oil import because of the price crashing from 100 dollar a barrel to 45 dollar a barrel. Other commodities prices are at lowest. The inflation is low. This all means a favourable situation for lowering interest rates which will give room to India for spending to create infrastructure. Because of the likelihood of labour wages going up in China, India has a chance in sectors like textiles, garments and auto ancillaries.

The Government has realised the opportunity and are thinking to push the reform agenda but there are hurdles. GST Bill is the key to Government's reform implementation agenda and it cannot be passed without Opposition being board. Furthermore, the Land Bill and labour reforms also have to be taken up at the earliest. We also need to expedite public investments and non-plan capital expenditure.

The Political maturity across parties is disappointing but many of the reforms like direct benefit transfers, auction of resources, financial inclusion will cause short-term pain but in few years from now; economy will be more competitive. This looks like a time of turbulence but the chances of it becoming a systemic crisis are less.

There is no doubt that if world was to get another recession in United States or in global economy, there is extreme vulnerability because of recovery all around being very slow. This causes the countries to be reluctant to increase interest rates even after many years of quantitative easing. So if recession happens there are no tools on the monetary policy side available now.

India needs steps to broaden tax base because our fiscal problems are more from our revenue weakness than from more spending. The assets sales by Government have to be expedited. Even the government lands should be monetised.

We should also not think that collapsing oil prices are good from every angle because someone has to pay the price. And if it is the banks who pay the price because of erosion of their capital and earning power, it will not be good for global economy in the long run. Oil prices have to stabilise where they are good not only for consumers but also for producers.

India's goods exports is declining for last nine months and will keep declining next year as well became of weak global demand and fall in commodity prices, both. So India's growth has a termidable challenge of declining exports. The short fall in crude oil prices has also led to lowering of our petroleum products exports. The economists say that global supply demand mismatch will take atleast few more years to cleak. Developing countries which were main drivers of world economic growth last 2008 financial crisis, are now facing a difficult time. Agreed, India is sheltered, but it can't remain unaffected. Are our planners ready for that?

There is no doubt that India is a domestically driven economy with huge growth prospects where interest rates will be falling over a period of next three years. We also have very little exposure to China and collapse of Yen will affect us least. But it is also true that our domestic investor base needs to be broadened quickly if our dependence on foreign capital has to be reduced.

The Government has time but not too much of it. Next one year is crucial because if the global investors lose their interest and start pulling out the capital, we will have no story left. The country cannot remain focused only on better delivery while putting the policy on the backburner.

The reform initiatives other than what was blocked by continued disruption in Parliament are also on a slow movement like large subsidies of foodgrains and fertilizers. Even labour laws nationalisation is stuck up because trade unions all across have shown great resistance to the idea. The public sector banks are under-capitalized and have huge nonperforming assets (NPA's). The re-structuring of Food Corporation of India, privatisation of airports, power sector reforms all need to be done. This all, along with slowing world economy may not be good for India's economic growth. U.S. Fed. has not hiked the interest rates which is a myopic view and not good for global economy including India.

This is the time for some out of box thinking for the country. The world all around is extremely over leveraged and indebted place. The tool of deficit financing which was invented to increase Government expenditure for growth and public welfare has exceeded all its limits in every country. Besides that, the culture of consumerism has over taken the world causing even individuals to use debt recklessly without bothering about their capacity to repay. Can this situation continue forever? Can expansion of money or printing of currency without proportional increase in the production of goods/services last? Is not there a need to return to a saner philosophy of life whereby individuals develop a sensible framework for their needs. What all an individual or family needs? They need a place to live; with access to food, good health care, education, transport and opportunities for employment and rise in life. Do they need to horde wealth beyond their requirements? Should not there be a public discourse on basic needs and for giving up excessive wealth back into the system for public good? Can there be a clarion call by political or societal leadership for individuals and organisations to give up their excessive wealth or resources to the Government in a "fund to be used for infrastructure creation"? Can we think of closing down public sector units which are no longer relevant because of their private counterparts performing well in various sectors? Can we think of monetising all prime properties lying with public sector units, Government Departments and Armed Force/para-Military Units all over the country? There are examples of sick units like HVOC (Hindustan Vegetable Oil Corporation) whose lands are not only lying idle but have also been encroached and can actually fetch crores of rupees to Government exchequer. There are hundreds of such PSU's.

The biggest challenge to world economy seems to be from carbon fuels led economy which is no longer sustainable. These fuels are not only going to exhaust very soon, but they also cause huge pollution. There is need for alternative fuels for which Technologies are available now. The best part of alternative fuels like solar power is that they can lend themselves to decentralized production by households and communities which will lead to lots of savings because there will be no transmission losses and huge conservation of energy can occur in smaller grids. This can be such a beautiful model whereby individuals produce their energies; utilize what they need and give excess to grid which can be used by industry which will pay for this. This decentralized model will not only lead to an end of power crisis but also change the 'power structure' of the country. People will have more power. Communities will be strengthened. I could only think of power sector where this decentralized model can happen but one could think of this happening in other sectors as well. Production of maximum goods or services at lower levels in a decentralized model will help remove distortions of an over centralised concentration of power in the hands of Government. This needs to be thought out elaborately and could be a wonderful solution for many ills of political structure and economy as well. It is time for tangential thinking for India and may be for the world as well.

Similarly, there are vested interests in other sectors e.g. Pharmaceuticals which don't want alternative cheaper therapies to succeed. They have made research defined in such a manner that without expensive clinical trials nothing could be legitimately called an approved medicine. If Hahnemann would have bothered with this, there will be no homeopathy in this word! Can human greed be so overwhelming and addictive that Pharma Companies would only be motivated by the profits they seek and not bothered about saving more human lives by reduction of costs of life serving basic drugs? This sector of Public Health care needs another radical thinking. How do we do it?

There may be no rational basis for saying so but I am of the firm belief that next 4-5 decades of are going to be full of turmoil because there will be paradigm shifts in the power structure, redefining democracy, values of life, needs of life and rewinding of whole economic concept of a nation's growth model. For example, why there should be huge energy guzzler model of growth – why GDP can't be higher with a low energy consuming pattern, especially, for hilly areas or fragile habitats which should only have tourism, horticulture and forestry as the main activities and no manufacturing activity at all. These are just few ideas I have on the table for all of you to consider.

Sustainability has become such buzzword in global parlance but is it something very new to the Indian psyche? No, it is not so. Since the time immemorial, Indians have placed a lot of value on not wasting the resources and utilising them for the benefit of all. That was the rationale behind common property resources in villages and tribal areas, the joint family system where the family could take care of all the needs of everyone without much problem. This was what Gandhi ji mooted in his idea of back to nature and Deendayal Upadhayaya ji said in his 'Ekatam Manav-wad' philosophy of life which nation has simply forgotten all about.

Since last thirty years, I have been trying to understand "when the definition of good and bad is so clear; when everyone knows what is good not only for him or herself but also for his family and the society at large and the nation, why people do things which will ultimately lead to harm themselves or their families or society or nation? It has always been a mystery which I have been trying to resolve. It is a strange thing that religions across the world and even non-religious spiritual texts have been talking about what is ethically good for human beings to survive together on this planet. They have also been preaching secular values like truthfulness, transparency, honesty, limiting the needs; taking only whatever is required for happy life and donating the rest to needy people. Despite preaching these values, nothing much has happened all across the world. Still people are there who have billions of dollars or resources (for which they do not have any use) lying in their bank vaults or in the name of trusts and companies they have created. They will not use it for ameliorating the distress of others while they can clearly see that there are billions across the universe suffering for want of basic necessities. Why does this Happen? Is there something basically wrong with the human beings or do they feel happy when they see others suffering? Is the basic villainy part of the human nature? Are humans by nature greedy, acquisitive and possessive not wanting to part with their resources in favour of others who could just live a decent life or survive with the help of these resources? These were the questions which plagued me throughout my life as a citizen, as a human being, as a family man, as an administrator, I have tried to understand the answer from multitudes of sources like books, Authors, Saints, Godmen and world leaders or whosoever I have come across. The best answers actually have come from ordinary people and some of the very old texts which try to explain the basic nature of human beings.

We are on the brink of disaster. Even if this universe has capacity to expand forever and can provide infinitely to the geometrically progressing population; the discovery of newer resources takes time. It is not that easy and in the transition process; civilizations get destroyed. We are on the brink as a human race. Most exhaustible resources are already depleting fast because there cannot serve the existing populations (what to talk of increase in population over next 50 years). Search for newer forms of fuel, newer forms of food; medicines and potable water is on. But all said and done; we are not able to even search a planet or space where the ever increasing populations could be shifted. What is it then that could change the existence on this earth? It the human race doomed to be unhappy? OR; beyond the uncertainties of the future, exhaustion of resources; we could reinvent ourselves and share and exist together as a happy, ever enjoying race? That is the billion dollar question? Each world leader, each saint, each true human being concerned for the welfare of all has been searching for an answer or rather a panacea for a 'permanent change' in the mentality of human beings so that they could minimize their needs, be happy with what they have and share their excess resources with others who need it and all this without coercion of the State or anyone else.

The issue is how the best values could become the hallmark of living of each person because of his/her self interest and not because of a charitable approach. No one is going to help others if the pious way of living does not help that person himself. Self interest and survival is at the core of being of human race.

If the world is going to be reformed and was to become a better place for living, it is not going to happen with talks about it, won't happen by making training courses or giving discourses to others, it is going to happen by changing ourselves. We need to work an our own head and heart. We can only work an our own self. We change and the world changes. We need to discard all value judgements. We need to put our past in the past. We need to stop seeking. Instead we need to concentrate on being. This leads to actions – which are detached from ego. Karma gives way to Dharma of our ancient texts. There is no point in attacking or destroying your ego because even if it could be achieved it serves not purpose. Only when we become aware of it – its ugliness gets revealed. We realize – that I don't have any need to control of master people or to keep them as any captives – because I am not insecure – I can see the violence in the concept of we vs. them – the foolishness of this divisiveness. Then the realisation occurs – peace of mind or clam or joy or happiness occurs by just letting all illusions go – and by being one with the rest of the world. When this realisation comes – I am not in the world – rather world is in me, I start doing things out of love pouring out of me. This all is part of our vedic texts, our folk lore – we have all forgotten it by creating a foolish duality called physical or material world and another spiritual world. In fact there is no such duality in real life. Once this awareness comes; sustainability will be an automatic choice; hoarding/greed/fear/anger/violence will become unnecessary and world will do all right-things. This is our heritage. Instead of speaking about it and trying to impress foreigners with it, we should practice it at individual level/society's level/ national level. World will take care of itself!

This is a topic may be I will explore in my next book but in the meanwhile let us hope that we humans will not destroy the planet and rather be able to live joyfully in it and India will successful foray the world into the 22nd century of peace and joy. Amen!